GRITS, GRACE, AND GOODNESS

GRITS, GRACE, AND GOODNESS

Smyth & Helwys Publishing, Inc.
6316 Peake Road
Macon, Georgia 31210-3960
1-800-747-3016
©2003 by Smyth & Helwys Publishing

Library of Congress Cataloging-in-Publication Data

Wellborn, Charles
Grits, grace, and goodness / Charles Wellborn.
p. cm.
ISBN 1-57312-410-9 (alk. paper)
1. Theology.
2. Baptists—Doctrines.
3. Christian ethics—Baptist authors.
I. Title.
BX6332 .W45 2003
230'.60—dc21

2003000840

CONTENTS

INTRODUCTION

If the meaning of life could be contained in a sentence,
there would be no need of telling stories.
—Henry Van Dyke (adapted)

A perceptive commentary bound with a personal story is to be cherished precisely because life is short and complex. *Grits, Grace, and Goodness* represents the faithful testimony of one pilgrim as he shares the fruit of a capacious Christian mind. It is the saga of a man well-born, with gifts, abilities and awareness far beyond average.

These gifts opened opportunities to the lad from the piney woods of Texas who became championship college debater, ski-troop soldier, boy-wonder preacher, national radio speaker, university professor, and citizen of two different English-speaking worlds. A minister's compassion and a prophet's responsibility have seasoned his life and work since his early twenties.

I have known about Charles Wellborn most of my life, as people variously called him the finest preacher they had heard, the clearest voice of conscience among his generation of Baptists, and the best professor they ever had. But I did not meet him until he came to Samford University in the summer of 1999 for "Revival Revisited," a remembrance of the great southern youth revivalists, then in their seventies, who had touched so many lives just after World War II. Less intense and assertive than I expected, totally noncompetitive for attention or the podium, disciplined by age and experience, constrained by a greater modesty than most men of his attainment, he nevertheless

demonstrated his ability as a pulpit marksman, rightly dividing the truth and allowing it to pierce the conscience, leaving his voiceprint on listeners' minds.

Rare these days is Dr. Wellborn's incisive reflection upon issues of faith, unfiltered by partisanship, nor mirrored in the language of Zion, nor telescoped into jive talk. The reader is compelled to follow the openhearted, open-minded oratory of the sermon, the candor of the essay, and the tenderness of the autobiography!

There is no denying that Charles Wellborn, child of the Southwest and the South, is from the land of grits. Grace came to him in forms beyond explanation—in wartime survival, in finding Christian faith, in the bonds of friends and family, in the bliss of an agile mind, and in dear colleagues. The goodness came to him recognizably from his Lord, the impact of home and family, the formative experiences of university years, the youth revival movement, the satisfaction of work well done. But goodness was also his to impart to those in need—in direct ministry, as university academic, as neighbor, and as friend.

If life cannot be reduced to a single sentence, and if "we will understand it better by and by," then *Grits, Grace, and Goodness* is an enormous help in the here and now.

Thomas E. Corts, President
Samford University
Thanksgiving 2002

FOREWORD

C harles Wellborn hit Baylor after World War II like a ton of bricks. He came back a decorated ski trooper. He was a brilliant student. He was a uniquely gifted speaker. He was a natural-born preacher. He was a native East Texan still completely comfortable with his roots and his values, his family, and his friends in spite of cruel war, broadening travel, sophisticated Europe, and hair-raising adventures. He stood out like a mighty oak in a mesquite pasture.

Like Venus on a summer evening, his first magnitude presence compelled both attention and respect. After an astoundingly impressive career in preaching, teaching, and university administration, it was natural for him, in retirement, to direct some of his prodigious energies into the kind of writing that has produced this book.

As the editor and publisher of *Christian Ethics Today* for more than five years, I enthusiastically welcomed every essay he ever submitted to me for inclusion in that journal. Our readers promptly embraced his regular offerings, and a fiercely loyal readership formed, attesting to the superior quality of his work.

The essays in this book reflect authentic Christian experience, impeccable Christian ethics, exceptional spiritual insight, admirable maturity, seasoned judgment, unaffected erudition, uncommon common sense, and genuine wisdom.

Read this book. Underline its passages. Read it again. Then go out to the bookstore and get extra copies to give to treasured friends.

Foy Valentine
Dallas, Texas
Fall 2002

Preface and Acknowledgments

The perceptive reader who comes to this material will immediately recognize that there is no true unifying structure to the volume. This is inevitable, since it is a collection of occasional pieces written or spoken over a period spanning many years. The reader will also be able to detect changes in ideas or understandings. I do not apologize for that. One's ideas and understandings inevitably change across the years—and ought to. I trust that the reader will also be tolerant of the fact, given the nature of this material, that there is now and again repetition in the text.

Although I am a professional academic, I have not written these articles primarily for my academic peers. I value their opinions, and I trust I have been academically respectable throughout, but I hope for a wider readership that includes not only clerics and professional religious workers but also the lay public, both those who are professing Christians and those who are not.

In an attempt to give the material some basic structure, I have organized the book into three sections. The first part deals with broader issues of the Christian faith and of general theology. Several of the articles in this section are based upon sermons delivered at various times and places, and they certainly carry the flavor of the pulpit and are shaped in terms of the audiences to which they were delivered. The second part of this volume includes articles dealing with more specific issues in the realm of Christian ethics—issues such as truth-telling, murder, the pleasure-principle, and various political, economic, and technological questions. Several are reflections of contemporary problems particularly important at the time when they were written.

Part three of the collection contains a single essay that I have titled "Credo." It is an attempt to summarize, after more than a half century of ministry as a preacher, pastor, and teacher, where my faith stands today. It is, in a real sense, my valedictory.

No thinker who dares to commit his ideas to print and the scrutiny of a reading public can fail to be aware of his indebtedness to manifold influences that have come to bear on his thought and experience. Many of those influences are unconscious and cannot be explicitly acknowledged. There is no way that I can pay tribute to them. Others are more explicit, and I have an obligation, as best I can, to recognize them here.

None of us can divorce ourselves from our educational experience, which is always relevant and crucial. My undergraduate study was at Baylor University in Waco, Texas, and it was a formative time for me. The overall Christian ethos of that institution meant much to me, but I must mention the lasting influence of men like Ralph Lynn of the Department of History; Leonard Duce of the Department of Philosophy; George Humphrey of the Department of Religion; and, perhaps most important of all, that academic ogre, A. J. Armstrong, of the Department of English, who bullied and loved me into a recognition that I should never for one moment be satisfied with anything I had accomplished to that point.

My first theological education was at Southwestern Baptist Seminary in Fort Worth, Texas. It was a crucial time for me, and I express gratitude for the influence and teaching of Stewart Newman, professor of the philosophy of religion; Robert Daniel, professor of Old Testament; Ray Summers, professor of New Testament; and, especially, T. B. Maston, professor of Christian Ethics, who deeply influenced all my future thought in this field.

My doctoral education was at Duke University in Durham, North Carolina. I was fortunate to sit at the feet of John Hallowell, professor of Political Science, and, in the Graduate School of Religion, Hans Hillerbrand, Creighton Lacey, and Waldo Beach. I must express special gratitude to Professor Beach, whose interest went far beyond the academic limits to invest itself in my personal and professional problems at a difficult time in my own life.

All of us are shaped intellectually by those thinkers whose ideas have helped to form our own perspectives. Those who are familiar with the works of the Niebuhr brothers, H. Richard and Reinhold, cannot fail to see their formative

influences in my thought. Paul Tillich, the German-American theologian, has made a major impact. Perhaps most important of all is the work of Dietrich Bonhoeffer, the German theologian/martyr. I express my gratitude to them.

All my life I have been primarily a preacher, and there are preachers who have materially helped me to understand what Christian preaching is all about. Foremost among them is James Stewart, the late, great Scottish pulpiteer—in my judgment, the finest preacher I have ever heard in the pulpit. I not only studied with Dr. Stewart in New College, the University of Edinburgh in Scotland, but I followed him from church to church in Edinburgh as he preached in order to hear his sermons. His influence was compounded when he graciously took me into his home and his friendship, and that relationship remained an important component of my own existence until his death.

I must also acknowledge the impact of Carlyle Marney, a magnificent preacher/prophet, not only in terms of his pulpit work but also because of his personal friendship and guidance. When I was a student at Duke University, my pastor was Warren Carr of Watts Street Baptist Church in Durham, North Carolina. Warren is a perceptive preacher and a compassionate human being, and his ministry meant much to me.

Finally, in this area, I must acknowledge my more recent debt to the congregation of which I am presently a member, and to its pastor. Greg Earwood and Faith Baptist Church in Georgetown, Kentucky, have ministered to me in manifold ways. They are a courageous and prophetic church, and I owe them a deep debt.

I was privileged to be a member of the faculty of Florida State University in Tallahassee for almost thirty years. I must pay my tribute to Bernie Sliger, the former president of the University, for his consistent encouragement and support throughout my academic career. I am grateful for the friendship and intellectual influence of my faculty colleagues there, especially Paul Piccard and Douglas St. Angelo of the Department of Political Science, Eugene Tanzy of the Department of English, and my associates in the Department of Religion—Robert Spivey, John Carey, William Swain, Walter Moore, Richard Rubenstein, Leo Sandon, and the late John Priest.

Any individual is not only a product of academic and intellectual experiences but also of personal ones. One's close friends make deep impacts upon one's ideas and consciousness. Here I must first express my gratitude to a remarkable group of

young men and women. The individuals who, by the grace of God, were chosen to be part of the great Youth Revival movement of the late 1940s and early 1950s made a lasting contribution to my life and thought. Jack Robinson, Howard Butt, Bruce McIver, Foy Valentine, Ralph Langley, Jess Moody, Bo Baker, Dick Baker, Frank Boggs, Warren Hultgren, Bob Harris, Buckner Fanning, Eunice Parker, Ardelle Hallock, Billie Russell, and especially, the late W. F. Howard, our mentor and guide, have impacted my life in indelible ways. The story of this remarkable movement and of these equally remarkable individuals has been told in Bruce McIver's *Riding the Wind of God* (Smyth & Helwys, 2002). Each of them, in his or her own field, has made significant contributions to the kingdom of God. I am grateful to all of them.

Two of my coworkers have left their permanent mark on me. My secretary for the entire time I was a pastor in Waco, Robbie McClain, is a remarkable human being, and she has remained my friend and confidant throughout the years. When I was University Chaplain at Florida State University, the late Jean Blasberg was my faithful and efficient assistant. I would add to this list my special friends in Great Britain where I have spent the last twenty years of my life. Keith Geniau, Gary Symonds, Brian Ellis, and Mary Hall will never know how much their loyalty and association have meant to me.

One's family is always important. I was fortunate to have a godly father and mother who gave me the kind of childhood that many would envy. My sons, Gary and Jon, have demonstrated unswerving loyalty, love, and encouragement. My two sisters—both of them remarkable individuals in their own ways—have given me support and deep affection. Faye Robbins (and her husband, Wayne) and LaVerne Wentworth (and her late husband, Richard) have not always agreed with me theologically, but they have never wavered in their encouragement and tolerance.

A final word is in order. Many of the articles in this volume were first published in the innovative journal *Christian Ethics Today*, founded by Foy Valentine and now edited by Joe Trull. For their encouragement and willingness to publish my material, I am deeply grateful. As far as the publication of this work is concerned, Thomas Corts, Jr., president of Samford University in Birmingham, Alabama, deserves the most credit. Tom and I became friends in the latter years of my life, but that association has proved to be both productive and satisfying. I cannot begin to express my appreciation to him.

All of us are the final product of all those whom we have met and of the totality of our human experience. I have been remarkably fortunate.

Charles Wellborn
London, England
March 2002

I

1

GRITS, GRACE, AND GOODNESS

(This article was first published in Christian Ethics Today.*)*

I am a Southerner, born and bred. Across the years I have observed that first-time visitors to the "hallowed ground" of the American South undergo a number of culture shocks. One such shock in the first encounter with that omnipresent ingredient on the Southern breakfast plate—grits. Southerners take grits for granted, not so our Yankee friends.

Years ago a friend of mine from Massachusetts came to Tallahassee, Florida, where I was then living. On his first morning in town I picked up my friend at his motel where he had just eaten breakfast.

"What's that white stuff they put on your plate?" he asked. "That stuff that tastes like wallpaper paste and, if you leave it long enough, turns into concrete?"

My friend's question reminded me of an old story. A traveler, making his first visit to the South, stopped for breakfast at a roadside cafe in Georgia. From the smiling young Georgia Cracker waitress he ordered bacon and eggs. In a few minutes she brought his order to the table. On the plate were bacon, eggs, and grits. Puzzled, the man called the waitress and, pointing to the white glob, inquired, "What is that?"

"That's grits," the waitress replied.

"But I didn't order grits," the traveler protested.

The waitress had an explanation. "Grits ain't something you order. Grits just come."

"Grits just come." By some trick of mind those words remind me of grace—that mysterious, almost indefinable working of God

in human experience. Through the centuries Christians have struggled to under-stand the full meaning of grace. Seeking a terse definition, theologians have defined it as the "unmerited favor of God." Those words hardly begin to plumb the depths of the concept. Christians attribute their salvation and forgiveness of sin to "Amazing Grace." Even that is not enough. Christ died not only that men and women might be rescued from their hopeless human predicament, but also that his followers might have aid and assistance in their continuing struggle to be "good." We call that assistance grace.

Grace is not something we can bargain for or purchase. It cannot be triggered by repeating some magic incantation or carrying out a prescribed sacred ritual. Grace "just comes."

We are sometimes frightened by grace, for it often arrives at unexpected moments or in unlikely circumstances. We frequently find the workings of grace difficult to understand. It doesn't always seem to make sense. We play the part of the elder brother in the parable of the prodigal son, protesting to the father that his open-armed reception of the prodigal violates all the canons of reasonable common sense. We constantly forget that what we humans call "sanity" does not always accord with the "Divine Sanity" of God.

Clearly, Christians are called to the task of being "good" in every area of life, personal and corporate. Christian ethics, at rock bottom, is all about goodness, and we should never underestimate the difficulty of the assignment. "Being good" is a rough, tough, dangerous job.

In the seventh chapter of Paul's Epistle to the Romans, the Apostle makes a profound confession: "For the good that I would I do not, but the evil that I would not do, that I do." Paul obviously speaks here out of the depths of his own moral struggle. He points us to the two great difficulties in that struggle. It is often diffi-cult to know what is right, and even if we believe we know the good thing, the job is far from over. It may be even more difficult to do the right.

All of my Christian life I have puzzled over the implications of the ethical teachings of Jesus—the parameters of a truly good life. Some people seem to find these moral dimensions simple. They wear badges, asking "What would Jesus do?" and believe beyond doubt that they know the answer to that question. My experi-ence is different. I am constantly impressed by what I, and others, have called "the hard sayings" of Jesus.

Let me give a few examples out of many. Jesus said, "Love your enemy. Do good to them that persecute you." As a World War II combat veteran, trained and ordered in that conflict not to love my enemy but to kill him, I find that injunction disturbing. Jesus said, "If a man strike you on one cheek, turn the other." I wrestle with the seeming contradiction between that statement and my natural inclination to defend myself and my children against unjustified violence. Jesus said, "Let him who is without sin cast the first stone" and "Judge not lest ye be judged." Painfully aware of my own moral shortcomings, I find it uncomfortable to speak words of condemnation on my fellow human beings, whatever their transgressions. Jesus said, "If a man ask you for your coat, give him your cloak also." How does that fit in with the apparent necessity to provide for my own material needs and those of my loved ones?

Unhappily, I have no glib answers for these moral dilemmas. Indeed, I distrust the simplistic solutions and the exegetical cartwheels of those who explain to me that Jesus did not really mean what he seems to have said. In terms of loving our enemies, we are told, for instance, that the appropriate moral guideline is to hate the sin but love the sinner. This impresses me as an easy out for many people—a convenient moral escape hatch. In everyday life the sin and the sinner appear inseparable, and to claim to hate sin and love sinners allows some of us to twist the meaning of love into contorted shapes. Once we get our dirty human hands on the word "love," we can make the word mean what our baser nature wants it to mean. Thus, we are allowed to do misshapen things—things that seriously contradict the essence of God's love as revealed in Jesus Christ. In the extreme, for example, individuals who classify all abortions as grievous sins may hate that sin so much that they respond by murdering abortion doctors and blowing up abortion clinics, all in the name of God and "goodness."

True, most of us do not go to that extreme. But is not the difference between many of our actions and that one a matter of degree, and does not the extreme case at least raise the red flag of moral danger?

The truth is that all through Christian history, those people who have sought to take the words of Jesus seriously and to act on them at face value have been judged by most of the world as, at best, mentally unstable, and, at worst, insane. When Jesus willingly "emptied" himself and gave his life on the cross, he did what the world would call an insane act. Paul spoke of it as "the offense of the cross."

When Francis of Assisi divested himself of all his worldly possessions in order to identify himself totally with his needy and oppressed brothers and sisters, he violated all the standards of common sense. How does one make sense of the choice of Father Damien to submit himself to the perils of a deadly disease for the sake of a few miserable lepers, or of the decision of Albert Schweitzer to use his manifold literary, medical, and musical talents not for the advancement of his personal career, but for the needs of a few hundred African natives?

I have concluded that the moral teaching of Jesus constitutes what I would call "the ethic of the overload." Again and again we Christians make our "sensible" moral decisions, only to discover with a cold shock that the Jesus-ethic requires much more. When Jesus counsels us to "turn the other cheek," he is clearly ruling out a tit-for-tat, revengeful response. The "eye for an eye, tooth for a tooth" syndrome has no place in the ethic of love. Many of us believe that we can make a rational case for such restraint, at least in our one-to-one personal relationships. But Jesus seems to be saying that our laudable refusal to react violently is not enough. We must go further and, apparently, invite even more violence from the aggressor. We must actively demonstrate that absolutely nothing another person can do to us will destroy our love for that person as one of God's children. That's the ethic of the overload.

When we follow our Master's instructions to give our needy neighbor our coat, Jesus says, "Not enough! Give away your cloak also." The ethic of perfect love—the ethic of the overload—constantly demands from us more than human reason or common sense seem to justify. To respond adequately to that ethic requires a sort of reckless faith in the grace of God and, beyond that, the willingness to suffer personally as a result of our action.

This brings us back to that "Divine Sanity." We must remember our human limits. We are, all of us, enclosed in a box, bounded on every side by the restrictions of time and space. Those restrictions affect everything in our experience, including both our language and our logic. To make matters even more difficult, a pervasive moral corruption is at work in the box and in us. We cannot ignore the fact that evil taints us all. Christians believe that God, in an act of unlimited love, has invaded that box in the person of the Christ. God's invasion was carried out not only to achieve the salvation of the human race but also to confront men and women with the moral challenge of perfect, unqualified love. The "Word made

flesh" speaks ultimate truth. It transcends in incalculable ways the inadequate time-space language and understanding of a corrupted humanity. God's ethical language is the language of the moral overload. To be good, in the fullest Christian sense, is to live out a moral pattern that is defined for us from outside the box.

Where does all this leave the committed Christian who sincerely wants to be good? I have learned much from the teaching and example of Pastor Dietrich Bonhoeffer, the World War II German theologian. Faced with a choice between the demands of perfect love and the unspeakable evils of Nazi Germany, he finally entered into a plot to assassinate Adolf Hitler. He did not make that decision easily. He agonized over it. He chose to act with a painful recognition of his own limits. Assessing the concrete situation as best he could, he did what seemed to him the "most right" thing to do. But the knowledge of his own fallibility forced him to pray, even as he acted, "Father, forgive me where I am wrong and where I sin." His decision cost him his freedom and, eventually, his life. I believe he faced that terrible personal outcome with a sure reliance on the overshadowing grace of God.

As men and women living in a fractured world, we do not have the option to be moral spectators. We must choose and we must act, often without any final certainty that we are totally right. Because our God-given fate is to be creatures of free will and choice, our responsibility in the face of the ethic of the overload is dismaying. Nevertheless, that confrontation is necessary if we are to make any progress toward the goal of being good human beings in a good society. Our choices cannot be made solely on the basis of a rational, mathematical calculation of "the greatest good for the greatest number," viewed through human eyes. Neither has God supplied us with a moral rule book. We cannot find our answer by referring to page twenty-four, paragraph five, subsection fourteen. To think like Jesus, and then to act upon those thoughts, is a dangerous and difficult task.

I am writing these words during the week just after Easter. In my meditations on the events of Passion Week, I am struck by the profound gap between two of the last sayings of Jesus on the cross. An awful moment comes when Jesus enters into the full despair of the human condition, crying out, "My God, my God, why have you forsaken me?" (Make no mistake; Jesus was not play-acting. His despair was real.) Yet, not long after those terrible words, he faced the final moments of his human existence with calm confidence: "Father, into your hands I commend my spirit." What filled that awesome gap and gave him strength? Somehow hope and

assurance arose out of despair. It was grace that made the difference, and that grace is still at work in our world.

We cannot command or manipulate grace. Grace "just comes." What we can do is be open and receptive to its coming. How can we be most open to grace? When we strive within our human limits to be the kind of men and women God wants us to be—when we struggle to be "good"—we are in a prime position to hope for those unexpected visitations of grace. This is not a "religion of works." All our imperfect works cannot justify us in the sight of God, but genuine faith produces good works, and God's grace is always waiting to be unveiled.

It does not appear to be our destiny to achieve perfect love here on earth. That culmination awaits the time when we are released from our time-space box and see truth and virtue, not as "in a glass darkly," but "face to face." Meanwhile, our task is to take seriously the demands of the moral overload. Relying always on grace, we must dare to act—to do in each concrete moral situation what seems the "most right" thing to do, even as we pray, "Father, forgive me, for I know not what I do."

2

LIFE'S BRILLIANT MOMENTS

(This article is based on a sermon delivered in the pulpit of the First Presbyterian Church, Tallahassee, Florida.)

I suppose that you have shared with me the experience of walking across a pitch-black room in the middle of the night, perhaps toward a light switch on an opposite wall. Outside the thunder roared and the rain beat down. Now and again brilliant flashes of lightning illuminated the countryside around you and through the windows brightened the dark room as if, suddenly, it were daylight. As you made your way across that room, perhaps you stopped and waited for the flashes of lightning, and when the room was bright, you got your bearings and made your plans to move without kicking a chair with a sensitive big toe—moving in the light, waiting when the darkness came.

It is against something of this background—though less prosaic—that one ought to read the twelfth chapter of the Gospel of John. John records that Jesus had been speaking to a group gathered around him. He was seeking to impart to them his conviction that within a brief period of time the end of his earthly ministry would come. He predicted an ignominious and disgraceful end, for he was to be executed as a common criminal. But in that death and what was to follow, Jesus believed that the meaning of all eternity was involved. As he sought to convey these things to his listeners, the Scripture records a strange event. The people reacted in different ways. Some thought it had thundered; others thought that an angel had spoken; perhaps only Jesus himself believed that it was actually the voice of God. In the poignant wonder of that moment Jesus uttered the

familiar words, "And I, if I be lifted up, will draw all men unto me." The people did not understand what he meant. Even his disciples were puzzled. They could not conceive of a crucified Messiah. They asked their wondering questions. Jesus seized the moment to say, "While you have the light, believe it. Walk in the light that you may be the children of light." Jesus urged them to take advantage of his presence, to walk in the light, for the darkness was soon to come.

I believe the words of Jesus are just as pertinent today as they were two thousand years ago. The insightful moments of life for you and me do not shine like some continuous noonday sun. Life's brilliant moments, at least for me, are rare and infrequent. They come and go like the lightning flashes in that darkened room. When they come, life and reality are illuminated for a brief moment. We are given a glimpse of truth. Then we sink back into the familiar twilight, into the blurred and uncertain visions of everyday. What happens in those brilliant moments, those moments of insights that now and then come to us? Suddenly, everything is clearer—the meaning of life and the reality of God. In those moments we may be able to gain a better knowledge of who God is and who we are. We are able to peer more deeply into the meaning of life itself. We are able to see our own possibilities, to see what we could be, given the grace of God. But how easy it is to let these brilliant moments slip by and even to let them pass unnoticed. We let them go. We fail to seize upon them. We fail to realize them for what they are. We let them become meaningless and unimportant in our everyday lives.

Victor Starbuck has put it in poetic words:

> One asked a sign from God; and day by day
> The sun arose in pearl, in scarlet set,
> Each night the stars appeared in bright array,
> Each morn the thirsting grass with dew was wet,
> The corn failed not its harvest, nor the vine.
> And yet he saw no sign.
>
> One longed to hear a prophet; and he strayed
> Through crowded streets, and by the open sea.
> He saw men send their ships for distant trade,
> And build for generations yet to be,

He saw the farmer sow his acres wide,
But went unsatisfied.

One prayed a sight of heaven; and erstwhile
He saw a workman at his noontide rest.
He saw one dare for honor, and the smile
Of one who held a babe upon her breast;
At dusk two lovers walking hand in hand,
But did not understand.

Life's brilliant moments: sometimes so prosaic, so ordinary, and yet suffused with the light and the power of God. If we would but seize them, as in a darkened room when the lightning flashes, get our bearings, see our obstacles, walk more nearly as we ought to walk.

When do these brilliant moments come—these moments of truth? There is no formula. They come like the wind, and we know not whither they come or where they go. They come to every person in his or her own way. God deals with each of us on our own level and according to our own understanding. The relationship of God to each individual is a unique and personal thing. Sometimes the brilliant moment comes, as it seems to have with the poet Starbuck, as we gaze upon the beauties of nature. I am no nature worshiper. I am too conscious of the cruelties of nature—the "tooth and claw" of real natural life. I think an individual can go far astray when worshiping indiscriminately the beauties of nature. I am a worshiper of the God who created that nature, with all its anomalies, and everything that God made points a finger to God, if properly understood, as the Apostle Paul argues in the first chapter of the Epistle to the Romans.

Sometimes the brilliant moment comes when we are overpowered by the majesty of God's created world. I stood late one night on a mountainside in Switzerland. The rest of my party were asleep in their rooms in the little hotel in the village of Zermatt, perched just at the base of the mighty Matterhorn. I was able from where I stood to see the moonlight catching the slopes of the snow-clad mountain. Everything was quiet around me except for the wind, and I felt that I could almost reach up to touch the stars. Then a cloud passed away and the moonlight reflected in total splendor the peak of the Matterhorn. The grandeur of

the world was there, and God, for me, was near. In such a moment God's lightning flashes into the soul. I was transfixed. Mystical—yes. Mysterious—yes. Unbelievable—no. It was too real, too vital, for me ever to forget it or deny it.

Sometimes the brilliant moment happens unexpectedly in the midst of calm and lonely meditation. Have you ever read late at night, when the rest of the family were fast asleep, when the world was totally still around you, and you were immersed in the thought of some writer? All of a sudden, as you sat alone, your mind fixed on what this person had written, seeking to comprehend it, you were caught up in the knowledge of a Presence there in the room with you, and in one brilliant moment you recognized the Divine.

It was that way with Thomas Chalmers, the great Scot preacher of another generation, who sat in his study in his church at Kilmarny, Scotland—the same study where for year upon year he had prepared his dull, dry, dusty sermons proclaiming a cold, formal, dead religion. But this one time, as he read his books and scribbled upon his pad of paper in the late night hours, suddenly God was real to him. Chalmers came out of that brilliant moment, out of that flash of lightning in his soul, to preach for the rest of his life the reality of a Christ who is alive, who is vibrant, whose spirit throbs with the beauty and wonder and energy and power of God. Life's brilliant moments!

Sometimes the brilliant moment comes in a time of sorrow, when suddenly the world collapses around us and the roof seems to fall in. Our ordinary world is shattered by the winds of loss or disaster. Through the cracks in the clouds of tragedy the light streams through. In that moment of total loss, when all earthly things seem useless, when only God remains, sometimes the lightning flashes. Some years ago I sat at the bedside of a dear young friend of mine. In the prime of his life he had been struck down by a deadly and fatal disease. I sat and gazed at his wasted body and tried to say, uncomfortable and uncertain as I always am in these situations, some words of comfort. My friend stopped my mumbling, incompetent words to say, "It's all right. I know what you want to say. But I have confidence in the God who saved me and who has guided me through my life. I trust him for whatever the future holds."

I was humbled. "I know not what my future holds, but I know who holds my future." Those are trite, oft-quoted words. Nevertheless, they contain the essence

of faith. My friend had had his brilliant moments and they were sufficient to sustain him, even unto death.

I think it was that way with Isaiah, in the Old Testament. He was a young courtier, a prince in the House of Israel. He sat down to write, "In the year that King Uzziah died . . . ." In that moment when his idol, his king, his master, to whom he had devoted all his services and his loyalty, went down into the grave, he records, "I saw the Lord." The lightning flashed, the brilliant moment came, and Isaiah saw and acted upon it.

Sometimes this moment may come in a crowded worship service, when the people of God come together in God's house. The glorious music of the church rings out, and the word of God is read and preached. Suddenly the spirit of God can be so real that all else fades away, and there is nothing left but the Risen Christ. I remember such a moment for me in the summer of 1946, soon after I became a Christian. I had the opportunity to attend a national meeting of Christian students held on the campus of the University of Kansas. One evening the speaker was, of all people, a United States Congressman. He spoke in terms of American foreign policy and the insights he felt his Christian faith had given him. He talked for an hour and fifteen minutes. When he finished, I glanced at my watch. I thought he had spoken for about twenty minutes. In the midst of his talk, and I think almost independently of what he was saying, suddenly God reached down to me and the lightning flashed in my soul. I wanted to leap to my feet and shout, "Hallelujah! Hallelujah!" God was there. It was a brilliant moment.

The poet Robert Browning understood all of this. His words are these:

> I stood at Naples once, a night so dark
> I would have scarce conjectured there was earth
> Anywhere, sky or sea or world at all:
> But the night's black was burst through by a blaze . . .
> There lay the city thick and plain with spires,
> And like a ghost disshrouded, white the sea.
> So may the truth be flashed out in one blow.

Life's brilliant moments!

What shall we do when the moment comes? Often it is upon us almost before we know it. We cannot predict it. We cannot manipulate or control it, which offends the "control freaks" of this modern world. The moment is here only briefly, and then the twilight closes in. What shall we trust? Shall we trust the vision of the brilliant moment, or shall we trust the more familiar twilight? Shall life be directed by what we see at our best, or by what we see in the mediocre, ordinary times of life?

Jesus left no doubt, for he said, "Believe in the light, for the light is real, and the light is true. The darkness is false, and in the darkness we walk astray. Believe in the light, and while you have the light, walk in it. Take your bearings then, and walk by those bearings." In that brilliant moment what did you see of the Lord? Believe it! In that brilliant moment, what did you learn of grace and love? Trust it! Live by it! In that brilliant moment, what did you see of yourself? What did you discover of your own sin and your own need? What did you discern of your own potential and possibilities? By the grace of God, seize the moment, believe in it, live by it, walk according to it. Do not doubt the flashes of God's lightning. Doubt rather your gloom, your depression, your hopelessness. Doubt your doubts, and believe in the God who gives spiritual insight. Walk in the light!

In his brilliantly written minor masterpiece, *The Screwtape Letters*, C. S. Lewis recorded a series of letters written by a senior devil named Screwtape to his junior apprentice, Wormwood. To Wormwood has been given as a special responsibility a "patient," a man on earth whom it is Wormwood's duty to tempt, distract, and confuse, to draw along the road toward Hell in the power of Satan, to prevent from coming into grace and right relationship with what Screwtape calls the "great enemy," God and his son Jesus Christ. Screwtape tells Wormwood, advising him of the course he ought to follow in his task, of an experience he had with one of his own "patients," a man whose thought patterns were thoroughly atheistic and who considered himself literate, logical, and intelligent.

Screwtape says, "One day I had him safely reading at the British Museum. He sat at a table immersed in the book of some man's meanderings called philosophy. But suddenly a train of thought began in that man's mind, and I sensed immediately that it was a train of thought that would lead him directly to the enemy. And suddenly the enemy, as is always his habit, was at the man's elbow, moving him along that path." The lightning began to flash; spiritual knowledge began to come;

and suddenly all the work of the demons for all those years was in danger of being swept away.

Using the masterful skills that had been taught him by his father, the devil, Screwtape did not argue with the man. Instead he stirred up his stomach and reminded him that it was almost lunchtime. He got him out of his chair and out of the library and into the street. And when the man had seen the passing crowd and heard the honk of buses and taxis and smelled the cigarette smoke and felt all of the rush of life about him, he pulled himself up and shook himself awake, reminding himself that this, after all, was what was real. The brilliant moment in which God began to speak was but an illusion. And Screwtape concludes, "And long ago he was safely in our father's Hell."

Life's brilliant moments! They are moments of insight, moments of knowledge, moments when we see ourselves more clearly as the sinners we are, when we see God as the God of grace and glory, when we see the cross of Christ for what it means in terms of salvation, compassion, and brotherhood. Jesus said, "While you have the light, believe in it, walk in it, act upon it; do not let it go."

For some who read this, this moment may be one of life's brilliant moments. In a bit we will all be outside again. The sun will beat down, the cars will go by, the crowd will talk of ordinary things. We will gather around the luncheon table or at the cocktail bar. I affirm to you that I believe the brilliant moment is more real than all of that. It is truth and life and eternity. While you have the light, walk in it!

3

THE BIRD IN THE SANCTUARY

(This article is a revision of a sermon preached in the Chapel at Duke University, Durham, North Carolina, and in the Schwab Auditorium at Pennsylvania State University, State College.)

On a Sunday morning a number of years ago I was scheduled to preach to a congregation gathered in a lovely and impressive sanctuary—one with stained-glass windows, high beamed ceilings, and rich carpets. As the church's pastor and I came into the pulpit to begin the service, we noted something that many others have probably witnessed at one time or another. A bird had somehow found its way into the sanctuary.

The bird was fluttering back and forth, high up under the ceiling beams. From time to time it threw itself frantically against the stained-glass windows, seeking a way out, only to be thrown back helplessly. I suppose it would have more symbolism if the bird had been a dove; actually, as I remember, it was probably a woodpecker.

I think anyone can easily imagine what happened. We sang the hymns—and watched the bird. We prayed—and some of us did "pious peeking" and watched the bird. I tried to preach—and the congregation watched the bird. After the service had been dismissed I mustered up my courage to inquire of the pastor, "Why didn't we just stop the service and get the bird out of the sanctuary?"

The pastor was embarrassed by the question. He replied, "Oh, I thought about doing that, but I just hated to interrupt what was going on!"

To me, that simple incident—a bird in the sanctuary—became a kind of double-barreled fable, an acted parable with both a major and a minor emphasis.

The minor emphasis is, I think, obvious. The pastor did not interrupt the service because he hated to disturb "what was going on." What was going on? We were engaged in the mechanics of religion, the activities in which decent, respectable people engage when they go to worship, the identifiable religious activities—singing, praying, preaching. It had become so important to this pastor and, I suspect, to many others like him, to go through the motions of religion that he could not bear to interrupt them, even when something had happened that destroyed much of their meaning and effectiveness.

Is this not the situation in much of the church today? Are we not often concerned so deeply with the "motions"—whatever our particular version of those motions may be—that we see them as ends in themselves? Our particular motions may be traditional acts of worship, or they may be more modern activities, such as study groups, meditation seminars, or interminable dialogue sessions. They become entrenched and so important in themselves that it is sacrilegious to interrupt them, even when they serve as superficial substitutes for life and action.

That was, for me, the minor impact of the parable. The major thrust is both more subtle and more important. That bird in the sanctuary, throwing itself helplessly against the windows, seeking an exit to the world outside, is a potent symbol of much of the modern church. I do not mean the church as an ecclesiastical institution, or as a rat race of organizational activism, or as an aesthetic enterprise, showing off its architecture and its music, or as a social service enterprise. I mean the church as it was founded to be—the living body of our Lord, pulsing with power and the potential of both physical and spiritual redemption. This was the New Testament church, turning a pagan world upside down.

Unhappily, this church is too often locked away in our ornate and costly sanctuaries. Having efficiently and safely incarcerated the church, we then come once or more a week with pious mien and stately step to visit it. Many of us "go to church" as we would go to a religious museum. For an hour or so we pay our respects, and then, church over, we go back out into the real world, back to where we live and work and play, leaving the church imprisoned within stones and steel and stained-glass windows.

Perhaps the difficulty lies in the fact that we talk much and easily about the church. We sometimes use terms so glibly and frequently that they become like old coins, passed from hand to hand until the inscriptions are rubbed off and it is no

longer possible to determine their value. It is essential for the man or woman who seeks reality in religious faith to understand what the church is in its essence. The New Testament used several metaphors to describe the church, but the most powerful and descriptive is that we have just employed—the church as the body of Christ.

It is possible for us to think of the church as a building, an organized institution, or a program of activities. If we so conceive of the church and if we are honest and sincere in our religious commitment, we may end up, as many contemporary Christians have, giving our ultimate devotion to a structure, an institution, or a calendar of activities—the tragedy described by someone as "first-rate loyalties to second-rate causes." Some years ago I sat in a local church conference in which members considered a moral issue cutting to the heart of the church's self-understanding of its nature and mission. The question was hotly argued. Finally one man—a good man—rose to make his comment: "We have discussed this question now for some time without mentioning our major concern. We must remember that we have a million dollars worth of property on this corner, and we must be certain, whatever we do, that we protect the church's investment."

Do you see what had happened? A good man with honest intentions had so misunderstood the meaning of the church that he had wrapped his spiritual commitment around bricks, plaster, and mortar. He had forgotten that, important as the protection of a church's property is, there is something more important: to do the will of God, to let the church, as the body of Christ, be the church—alive, powerful, and redemptive in the world.

Not really different in orientation are those who see the church not as a building or a program, but simply as people, grouped together for a common purpose. My own denominational tradition has a time-honored definition of the church as "a body of baptized believers, banded together to worship and serve God." However valid this definition of the local church body in its institutional function may be, it becomes demonic if one gets "hung up" on it or accepts it as the last word. For if this is the essence of the church, then the church is human-made, just exactly as if it were a building.

For multitudes today the church is a group of people who choose to associate themselves together for laudable purposes—one good organization among many in the community. It fits neatly in with civic clubs, fraternal organizations, and

charitable concerns. One picks a church to join in the same way that one might pick a country club—because it is in the right part of town, has attractive facilities, provides good music, has a personable minister, and includes congenial people in its membership. Churches strive for good fellowship, which often means that they consist of people we enjoy seeing frequently and with whom we share a whole complex of common interests, economic, political, and social.

This is to miss the whole dynamic of the church or, at least, the church portrayed in the pages of the New Testament. The primitive church is never depicted as a group of people who got together because they liked each other. I have never been convinced, for instance, that Peter and Paul "liked" each other. The evidence is that they irritated each other intensely and seldom if ever agreed on major issues. The New Testament describes the pattern of a church made up of people who did not necessarily like each other but were able to find something that transcended their differences and bound them together in a common calling and a common task. This is a bond far stronger than mere fellowship.

Our Lord said, "Upon this rock I will build my church, and the powers of death shall not prevail against it" (Matt 16:18). The foundation rock is the incorporation of women and men into the body of Christ. I submit that not only the powers of death, but far less frightening forces are constantly prevailing today against the church as a bureaucratic organization, a building, a program of activities, a hierarchy, a denomination, and a group of like-minded people.

What then is the church? It is the body of Christ, divinely and supernaturally called into being by the creative and redemptive grace of God. Human beings do not finally build it, or organize it, or promote it. Into it men and women of faith are mystically incorporated. They are in evangelical terms "born again." Christ is the head of the church, and those who commit themselves to him are made one with him—we in him, and Christ in us. We are spiritually alive; we are the concrete manifestation of Christ in the world. Where we are, there is the church—if it is anywhere.

What does this realization imply? It means simply that we cannot leave the church in the sanctuary when the worship services are concluded. We are the church, and wherever we are—at home, in an office, in a classroom, in a restaurant or bar, on a farm, or in a factory—there is the church. It is spiritual delusion to believe that we can go to church or leave church, putting on or taking off the

church like an old overcoat. We are the church or, at least, if we are faithful men and women, we are seeking to become the church.

The question I ask here is simple and to the point. I inquire as to the state of the church but not the church in its cathedrals, meeting houses, or chapels. I am asking about the church where you and I live. How goes it with the church in your kitchen, your shop, or your place of business?

When theologians discuss the marks of the true New Testament church, they most often talk about such matters as the proper observance of the sacraments or ordinances, the polity of the church, its doctrine, and its practices. Too often, we neglect the even more basic marks of the church as it functions in the world, characteristics that are emphasized in the book of the Acts as it describes the life of the early church. It is significant that while this scriptural material has little to say about doctrines, sacraments, ordinances, or polity, it has much to say about more elemental things. If we are to be the church, wherever we are, how do we test the spiritual health of the church we are becoming? What are the marks of the authentic church?

Wherever the church is, there is love. Precisely to the extent that the church does not live by love, it misses the mark of authenticity. The early church made no claims to out-organize, out-promote, out-build, out-manipulate, or even out-think anyone else. It did promise to out-love everybody else. The hostile world in which it found itself marveled that these women and men of faith out-loved the pagan world. Their love reached out to embrace those who did not accept the church's doctrinal teaching, as well as to human beings of both genders, all races, and every economic or social status. From a New Testament standpoint an individual can repeat all the right creeds, believe all the right doctrines, go through all the right religious "motions," discourse learnedly on everything from Barth to Buber, but if he does not love, he or she is not the true church in the world.

Wherever the church is, there is service. Service is love in action. I mean here concrete service, blood-and-sweat service, forcing one to become involved in the concrete suffering of the world about us. That world is presented not abstractly, but specifically in the person of the nearest human being in immediate need.

Years ago, when I served as Chaplain to the University, part of my responsibility was to act as liaison officer on the campus for two government programs, the Peace Corps and Vista. I interviewed dozens of students who were interested in

investing a year or more of their lives in those programs. Most of the students I talked with came out of religious backgrounds—Catholic, Protestant, Jewish, and others. I heard them say over and over again, "All my life I have heard people talk about service. Preachers preach about it, we sing about it, we pray about it, my professors in the classroom lecture about it, we study about how to serve. I have had enough of talk. I want to get my hands dirty in human need. I want to do something for somebody in a way I can see and touch and feel." It seems to me that there is the essential impulse of the church to serve.

Where is the church as the body of Christ? Is it only where we talk, sing, and pray, or can it be found beyond the religious motions—wherever individuals give themselves in honest, decent concern for the needs of other human beings?

Wherever the church is, there is witness. This is surely one of the authentic marks of the true church, the church as the body of Christ, alive and powerful for human redemption. In the book of Acts we are told that "The Lord added to the church daily such as should be saved" (Acts 2:47). Christians loved, served, and witnessed, both in their personal lives and by their words. Thus, they thrust themselves into the lives and destinies of others. Witness must be by both act and word, for the act finds its expression in the word, and the word is the translation of the act. If we are becoming the church, we are becoming witnesses. "I will make you," said Jesus, "to become fishers of men."

Love, service, witness—these are the real marks of the authentic church, the church as the body of Christ, alive and powerful. But if the church is to love, serve, and witness, it must somehow break loose from the stone prison in which we have incarcerated it. It must take on flesh and blood. It must take seriously its commitment to the "follow-ship," not just the fellowship, of Jesus Christ. It must go where Christ is. And where is he? Is he not where he has always been, wherever there is suffering, sorrow, discrimination, misery, hunger, loneliness, and despair? He stands in the midst of life in all its brutality, injustice, and sin, saying, "Come unto me."

Can we follow him? Can the church be the church? Do you remember that bird—that helpless bird throwing itself against the stained-glass window? Is it not time—high time, urgent time, almost perhaps too late—to smash those stained-glass windows, pull down the heavy oaken doors, and let the church loose in the world?

4

SKATING ON THIN ICE

(This article is a revision of a sermon preached in the Chapel at Cornell University, Ithaca, New York.)

I n a disturbing essay titled "This Present Age," the nineteenth-century Danish theologian Søren Kierkegaard characterized the reflective, over-intellectualized society of his day in a profound parable. He wrote:

> If a jewel which every one desired to possess lay far out on a frozen lake where the ice was very thin, watched over by the danger of death, while, closer in, the ice was perfectly safe, then in a passionate age the crowds would applaud the courage of the man who ventured out, they would tremble for him and with him in the decisive action. . . . But in an age without passion, in a reflective age, it would be otherwise. The crowds would go out to watch from a safe place, and with the eyes of connoisseurs appraise the accomplished skater who could skate almost to the very edge (i.e., as far as the ice was still safe and the danger had not yet begun) and then turn back.

If the skater accomplished this with a flourish and a certain style, the crowd would applaud and honor him with a magnificent banquet. No one would recall that after all, since he always stayed where the ice was safe, the hero had never risked anything, nor would

many bother to remember that, after all, despite all the flourishes and all the cheering, the hero had never come close to the precious jewel.

By "a passionate age," Kierkegaard seems to have meant a time in which people of faith and commitment would dare to risk everything, even their lives, for the sake of that in which they believed. I think it is a legitimate judgment that the time in which we live is largely an age without genuine passion, or perhaps better, a time of pseudo-passions. People seem willing to risk a great deal for goals like material success or political power, but there are rare examples of those who are willing to live recklessly in the name of ultimate truth.

This is an artificial, dehumanized age, and those of us who live in it—especially those of us who would like to refer to ourselves as committed Christians—need seriously to examine ourselves within its context. What is the nature of our commitment? How close has it actually brought us to the precious jewel, the "pearl of great price"? Many seem deeply concerned about doing their religious skating with a flourish, and they listen eagerly for the applause of the crowd. The essential question remains: Have we ever left the safe ice to go out beyond the limits where we are, in Kierkegaard's terms, "watched over by the danger of death"?

In more recent times than those of the thinker whom some have called, like Hamlet, the "Gloomy Dane," another Christian has been used of God to pose the same kind of searching questions. Dietrich Bonhoeffer, the brilliant German theologian executed in a concentration camp before he was forty years of age, wrote in one of his letters from prison, "The day cries out for faith, and all men have is religion. How useless! How tragic!"

What Bonhoeffer agonized over was the failure of commitment. For him the universal and all-pervading crisis of existence had narrowed down to a prison cell, where suffering, degradation, bestiality, and the constant possibility of death were the fabric of experience. With fundamental reality drawn to a fine point, Bonhoeffer found that what we call religion—especially polished, refined, and cultured religion—collapses like a house of cards. Faith is fragile unless it rests upon a particular kind of commitment—reckless, unconditional commitment to the full reality of the God revealed to us in Jesus Christ.

I grant you that it is difficult for most of us, living as we do in a situation totally foreign to that in which Bonhoeffer found himself, to come to grips with the

dimensions of the kind of commitment he felt was essential. In our lives, most of which are, by comparison with Bonhoeffer's, cushioned, cottoned, and comfortable, it is hard to push through to basic reality and to examine with honesty and insight the structure of our personal commitments. Yet our own spiritual uneasiness (something I find pervasive in modern Christianity), our own inner sense of failure revealed in those random moments of truth that invade our busy schedules, and above all the insistent pressure of God's Holy Spirit upon us demand that we do so.

We live in a world that is largely hostile to the basic assumptions and declarations of the Christian faith. It is a society that places its highest values on what can be seen, touched, or pleasurably felt, added up in neat columns of figures, or stashed away in safe-deposit boxes. We Christians perform our daily routine in a culture that is for the most part indifferent to any claim made to the relevance or reality of God. All about us is social strife, economic unrest, and moral rottenness. And, here we are, the church, huddled together, reassuring ourselves at regular seven-day intervals of our righteousness and our rightness. We are the committed!

I do not mean to overdramatize the situation, nor do I seek to exalt Christians as the potential nucleus of a band of besieged martyrs. Frankly, the secular world about us is not threatened by us enough to raise the banner of persecution. I do think, however, that the community of faith needs to recognize clearly the circumstances in which we stand and the relative position that we occupy.

We call ourselves "the committed." Are we? I am asking, of course, in terms of that vital life-or-death commitment to God in Christ of which Bonhoeffer spoke—that reckless skating on the thin ice that Kierkegaard described. More specifically, I am asking about that quality of commitment outlined by Jesus Christ when he called for a total love of God, worked out in a total love of the neighbor. If our commitment is to meet those standards, it must be rethought, refaced, remade, not just once, but continuously. What is the quality, the outreach, and the depth of our commitment?

By definition this kind of commitment can never be complacent. It is not really in the same family with the easy allegiance to religious creeds, organizations, or traditions professed by so many in our day. It has little or nothing to do with the surface trappings of religion, the dead forms of ecclesiasticism, or the fantastic squirrel cage of pseudo-religious self-improvement courses, purporting to show us

how to be easily happy and wealthy. Much of what makes up modern American church life is foreign to this kind of commitment.

Complacency is a symptom of superficiality, and superficiality always indicates a drastic warping of genuine religious faith. It is salutary to note that, outside of professional theological circles, it is almost impossible in today's world to stir up a genuine religious argument. If such an argument does arise, it is almost always about secondary issues. The truth is that few people today have any serious objection to God, the church, or theological doctrines; they simply deem the whole matter irrelevant and unimportant.

When I was a pastor, a young man came to see me in my office. He was soon to graduate from the university across the street, and he told me that he wished on the following Sunday to present himself to our congregation as a candidate for baptism. A clean-cut, intelligent lad, he frankly told me that his decision did not come out of any spiritual struggle or conviction. "I have decided," he said, "that in my life I want to be identified with the best people. I want to have a family, and I want my family to grow up within a church atmosphere. All things considered, I think it would be better for me to be inside the church than outside it."

When I sought to talk with him about the basic meaning of such a decision, I met a blank wall. He gave no evidence of any feeling of personal sin or the need for forgiveness, and he had no interest in the implications of a life-changing commitment to the Christian faith. I finally had to tell him that I could not conscientiously recommend him for membership in our congregation. He was not angry with this decision. On the contrary, the matter was simply not important enough for him to become disturbed. Later, I found his name in the list of additions to the membership of another church in the city. He had joined the ranks of the "camp-followers" of the church.

This generation could learn much from two men whose lives and beliefs were diametrically opposed, but who deeply influenced our intellectual world. Friedrich Nietzsche, the German philosopher, declared the "death of God" long before it became fashionable to do so, but he never made that declaration lightly. He recognized that he was proclaiming a catastrophic event, the end of an epoch, the dawn of a new and terrifying period in human history—and in his own life. He clearly foresaw the consequences of his declaration: without God, chaos. He deliberately chose chaos. While the choice may be incredible to some of us, we must recognize

that he made it with deliberate courage, without illusions, and realizing full well what he did. In no way was his choice complacent.

There was another towering figure in the nineteenth century. Feodor Dostoevsky, the Russian novelist, grappled with much the same set of problems as those faced by Nietzsche. While the German chose chaos, the Russian turned back to God in Christ. When some criticized his novel *The Brothers Karamazov*, Dostoevsky wrote, "The dolts have criticized my obscurantism and the reactionary character of my faith. These fools could not even conceive so strong a denial of God as the one to which I gave expression . . . the whole book is my answer to that denial. . . . . Thus it is not like a child that I believe in Christ and confess him. My hosanna has come forth from the crucible of doubt."

While Nietzsche and Dostoevsky walked the opposite roads of faith and non-faith, they shared a common understanding of the depth of the problem and the meaning of commitment. They ruled out easy, pat answers to the human predicament. They recognized that, in a crisis age, religion that rests for its authority upon worn-out tradition and liturgical cliches—upon what mother said, upon what the preacher said, upon what society thinks—will not do.

The Apostle Paul declared himself in concrete terms when he confessed, "I am Christ's slave." Colin Wilson, a fit spokesman for much of our age, writing in his book *The Outsider*, is nauseated by this. Modern man, he thinks, will be slave to nothing unless that slavery draws the line between Being and Non-Being.

And yet, is this not precisely where we who are of the faith stand? If our commitment is conceived of in Bonhoeffer's terms and if it is the commitment demanded by Jesus, then it is the difference between life and death, truth and error, light and darkness, order and chaos, meaning and gibberish, heaven and hell, God and no-God. It is a venture that takes us far beyond the limits of the safe ice.

If this commitment cannot be complacent, it also cannot be contractual. A contract is an agreement entered into by two parties, both of whom have certain rights, both of whom receive some benefits or compensation, and both of whom assume certain obligations. Each party to a contract spells out his or her own protections and limitations. Can a true commitment to God be on this basis?

Remember Jacob at Bethel in the Old Testament? I have always found it difficult to preach on "Back to Bethel" because, frankly, I am disgusted with Jacob. Rising from his visionary experience, Jacob cries out, "If God will be with me, and

will keep me in this way that I go, and will give me bread to eat, and raiment to put on . . . then shall the Lord be my God . . . and of all that thou shalt give me, I will surely give the tenth unto thee" (Gen 28:20-22). What Jacob is proposing is quite simply a contract with God, as if they were two equal partners in an equal agreement. "If God will do God's part, then I'll do mine. I'll bargain with God." How striking is the contrast with Thomas, the New Testament disciple, who, confronted by the resurrected Christ, cried out, "My Lord and my God."

New Testament faith-commitment involves casting oneself totally and unreservedly upon the mercy and grace of God. The philosopher Spinoza was right when he said that the man who truly loves God knows that we cannot expect God to love us in return. God owes us nothing and is under no contract to us. The blessings that arise from our commitment come purely from God's grace, not through any contractual obligation. In the words of the familiar hymn, sinful people can approach God in only one way:

> Just as I am, without one plea,
> But that thy blood was shed for me,
> And that thou bidd'st me come to thee,
> O Lamb of God, I come, I come.

One other negative dimension remains in the rethinking of our commitment. Such commitment can never be conservative. To embrace this facet of commitment is to cut across the pattern of a non-passionate age. We live in time that puts high value on security. What do most people want? Quite simply, we want to be like everyone else in our peer group, comfortable and safe. In *The Lonely Crowd*, David Reisman tells of interviewing a twelve-year-old girl about the comics. Her favorite comic strip was "Superman" because the hero of that series could fly. "Would you like to fly?" the interviewer asked. "Oh, I guess I would if everybody else did," the girl replied. "Otherwise, it would be rather conspicuous."

By all means, says the world about us, don't be conspicuous. Don't go off any deep ends. Be reasonable; be safe (never "half-safe"); be secure. The buzzword is "conform." With dry-cleaned brains and a preshrunk spirit, you can always get by. Be conservative!

The Christian, rethinking his or her commitment, must have trouble with that counsel. It does not seem to fit the reckless mood of the New Testament. The Apostle Paul advises us, "Be not conformed to this world, but be transformed by the renewing of your mind" (Rom 12:2). The truth is that Paul would be black-balled by our clubs, ostracized by our social crowd, or even denied membership in many of our churches. Few of us are attracted to oddballs out to change the world. We react against people who have a reputation for turning things upside down. Most of us have never even lighted up the tilt sign, and we are not eager to begin now.

Jesus said, "If anyone wants to follow me, let him take up a cross." That's nice to sing about, but a good many people think that anyone foolish enough to get himself crucified is obviously immature, foolhardy, and in need of some good stiff courses in social adjustment.

Still, underneath our smug cynicism and tight self-protection is a lingering sense of futility and a wavering sea of meaninglessness. Somehow we feel that we have missed something somewhere. Many of us are religious in the fashion of the day, but that is not enough. We talk the right talk, but there are ashes in our mouths. Is it that, with flourish and spectacle, we sweep out on the ice but never very far, never past that invisible line prescribed by safety, ambition, prudence, or self-interest? Is it that, in our honest moments, we see that our commitment lacks any element of dangerous involvement or risk?

Yet, if one looks back at the history of Christian church, it has rarely been the cautious, conservative, socially-acceptable individuals who have earned our veneration. The martyred Apostles, the early believers suffering cruel Roman persecution, and individuals like Francis of Assisi, Father Damien, Albert Schweitzer, Dietrich Bonhoeffer, or Martin Luther King Jr. could not have been characterized in any sense as safe and conservative. They all skated on thin ice, and most of them paid a terrible penalty.

Despite the deafening cacophony of this frantic age, those who have ears to hear can detect a distant pounding. If you listen carefully, you will realize that the pulsations are irregular, jumpy, uncertain. You are listening to the heartbeat of the world, and it is not a healthy heartbeat. It is the sound of a sick and broken culture. The cardiograms are in our morning paper or television newscast, in last week's issue of *Time*, in the apathy of our churches and the holy drone of our

preaching. Underneath the sophisticated crust of our contemporary age there is a raw reality. It is a time of crisis, testing, and judgment.

In response to that ragged heartbeat, we who are Christians are challenged to make our faith more than a Sunday saunter through a religious museum. We are commanded to skate on thin ice, to venture and to risk. Out where the ice is thin, death is indeed the watchman, but there is also a Pearl of great price.

5

"GO . . . PREACH!"

(This article is a revision of a message delivered to an interdenominational conference of Christian ministers in Bristol, Tennessee.)

Christians, like all human beings, are easy prey to the optimistic fallacy of pretending, even to ourselves, that things are not what they are but what we wish they were.

For example, it would be comforting if we were able to affirm with conviction that the church of Jesus Christ today stands firm and stalwart, proclaiming in steady and authoritative tones the good news of redemption, stretching out arms of strength and love and hope to all people everywhere. That is what we would like to say. Sometimes, especially when we are carried away by our own oratorical flourishes, this is what we do say. In all honesty, is this the pure truth?

How do we look not just to our own prejudiced eyes, but to that pagan, secular world outside the Christian circle? Here are the words of an intelligent and sympathetic observer who himself is not a Christian. True, the words were written years ago, but they are still perceptive.

> The churches face a dilemma which is a matter of life and death. . . . .
> They come down to us with a tradition that the great things are permanent, and they meet a population that needs above all things
> to understand the meaning and direction of change. No
> wonder their influence has declined, no wonder that men
> fight against what influence they have. Ministers are as
> bewildered as the rest of us, perhaps a little more so. . . . If the

churches really could interpret life they would be unable to make room for their congregations; if men felt that they could draw anything like wisdom from them, they would be besieged by bewildered, inquiring people. . . . It isn't indifference to the great problems that leaves the churches empty; it is their sheer intellectual and spiritual failure.[1]

We can say this evaluation is exaggerated, and in some ways it is. The churches are not always as bewildered and uncertain, nor as impotent, as this writer's judgment would imply. I suggest, however, that there is the sting of partial truth in these words and that they cut painfully close to the bone.

I suspect that those of us who are involved in the professional Christian ministry do wonder sometimes, "Is anybody listening to us?" We know we have something important to say, but are we saying it in a way that grips the hearts and minds of our listeners? Are we really getting through to people?

I would suggest that the answer to those important questions cannot be given simply in terms of religious statistics and ecclesiastical expansion. In this country— in vivid contrast to many other parts of what used to be called the "Christian world"—we have an abundance of "religion." Some of my friends from England who visit the United States for the first time marvel that there is a functioning church on almost every corner. But once we lay bare the quality and content of that religion, what do we discover? Here are the bright trappings of ritual, and there are the dead forms of pedantic ecclesiasticism. Here is ponderous and ever-multiplying organization, and there is pyramiding promotional enterprise, often without spiritual substance. Is this what speaks to men and women caught up in sin, guilt, doubt, crisis, and predicament?

And what of some other standards of church success? We parade the slick and efficient propaganda methods of Madison Avenue applied as "hidden persuaders" to bring people to some kind of—often almost any kind of—religious decision; the fantastic squirrel cage of religious self-improvement courses, in which we teach people to manipulate God so as to be rich, happy, and materially successful; the rat race of religious activism, in which decent and sincere people destroy themselves spiritually and psychologically in the meat grinder of services, committees, meetings, seminars, and conventions. Is this a vital ministry to a sick and dying world?

Twenty centuries ago Jesus commanded his followers: "Go . . . preach!" I maintain the proposition that a prime failure of the modern Christian church is its failure to obey adequately that command. I know there are many other defects in the church and in the Christian community. I know it is standard procedure for preachers and pastors to blame laymen and laywomen for their indifference, their lack of dedication, their poor stewardship, their spiritual insensitivity. But I believe that a pivotal center of the Christian mission is the pulpit, and the pulpit must bear a major responsibility for whatever is wrong with the church today. I say this as a preacher myself with a decade spent in the pastorate. Our churches have not failed Christ primarily in terms of organization, official or orthodox doctrine, money-raising, or programming. The rise of the so-called superchurch—an enormous religious bureaucracy striving through a multitude of activities to be all things to all people—is testimony to the fact that some of us have learned well the secular lessons of advertising and promotion, relying on the wisdom of the "spin doctors" to build ecclesiastical empires.

In spite of all this I sense that many of us live with a deep, disturbing sense of failure. What is the root of that feeling? I do not claim to have a total answer, but I do believe this: we have somehow failed in our preaching. "How then shall they call on him in whom they have not believed? And how shall they believe in him of whom they have not heard? And how shall they hear without a preacher?" (Rom 10:14). If our churches are to recapture the ear of the world, if we are to bring the gospel directly to bear upon the wounds, the sores, and the cancers of twenty-first-century individuals, we must somehow recover the lost and neglected ministry of the word, spoken with spiritual power and persuasion. Perhaps we must learn anew what it means to preach.

Some pastors may well ask, "What do you mean? Most of us are asked to do more preaching now than we can handle. Four, five, six times a week, we must prepare and preach some kind of sermon." This is true. The fact that there is so much sermonizing required of many of us inevitably drags down the quality of what we do. But let me emphasize something that most of us have repeated, sometimes thoughtlessly, a thousand times. Those who are called to the pastoral ministry are called to preach. Despite our recognition of that prime responsibility, we let a dozen secondary duties take precedence over the ministry of preaching. I do not disparage the importance of these other activities, but I do wonder how

much guilt most of us bear because of that to which we have subjected our congregations: the shoddy, second-rate, ill-prepared, unthought, unprayed-over trivia; the trite platitudes; the worn-out illustrations; the creaking, aged outlines; the three points, a sad story, and a poem that we have foisted on our helpless listeners. Surely there are more fruitful ways for church members to develop the patience of Job than having to sit through second-rate preaching Sunday after Sunday! There is some wisdom in the words of the cynic who observed that Christianity had proved its strength most strikingly by surviving its own preaching.

Surely this is not what Jesus intended when he commissioned us to go and preach. To proclaim the good news of redemption is the highest of all privileges. The Apostle Paul refers to it with powerful simplicity as "the holy calling." In that phrase there is some hint of the challenge of handling, Sunday after Sunday, the word, some hint of the venturesome daring, the exhilarating demand that is made upon God's man or woman in a Christian pulpit.

"Go . . . preach!" That is our imperative. But what does it involve? What are we to preach? The simplest answer is still the best, if we but understand all that it means: preach the gospel. There can be no valid Christian preaching apart from the proclamation of God's redemptive act in Jesus Christ. Preaching must always and invariably be biblical, for it is the Scriptures which set out for us the core of preaching, the kerygma—the events of salvation history, the life, death, burial, and resurrection of our Lord. Preaching is kerygmatic, or it is not preaching at all. It must always begin with this.

Make no mistake about it, however; it cannot stop there. There is no gospel without the kerygma, but the kerygma does not complete the gospel. To preach the gospel is to set the kerygma down in the midst of women and men, to bring it to bear with all its meaning upon human beings as they are, where they are. To proclaim the good news of God's saving act in Jesus Christ is to call people to repentance and faith, but it is also to call them to the lordship of the Risen Christ, effective in every area of existence and experience.

Here is where the water hits the wheel. Here is where gospel preaching becomes both relevant and revolutionary. The gospel preached in a vacuum, locked up in a church house, never disturbed anyone. I doubt that it ever saved anyone. The gospel preached in vital relationship to flesh-and-blood human beings with real problems—this becomes the message of redemption, the power of God

46

unto salvation. To preach is to confront men and women with the word in such a way that the word becomes a living Word, so that people are grasped in the midst of their human predicament by the power of Christ. They are faced with his love, humbled by his holiness, lifted by his everlasting arms, healed by his matchless grace, and transformed by his enveloping spirit. "If any man be in Christ, he is a new creation" (2 Cor 5:17).

Is this the kind of preaching we do—most of us—Sunday after Sunday? If it is, we stand in a proud heritage, the train of the prophets. But there are at least two convenient ways in which we allow society to stifle the prophetic witness of the Christian faith. One way is by capturing the faith and making it a defender of the current culture, a supporter of the status quo, a bulwark of a certain way of life and established order. When this happens, as if often does, the preacher becomes the "pet" of society, a number one citizen in the community, well cared for, undisturbed, free to play his religious games, never upsetting anyone. To be this kind of preacher is, quite bluntly, to be a "kept" preacher, the lewd and immoral mistress of an unbaptized culture. It is to sell one's birthright for a mess of pottage.

The world's other method is to encourage the church and the preacher to deal always with trivialities, to specialize in swatting gnats and be conveniently blind to camels. In this way we can enjoy the traditional ceremonies and comforts of our religion without ever being involved in genuine human experience. The preacher must be careful to avoid all burning issues. He must by all means refuse to preach on controversial subjects. He must amuse, entertain, soothe, and fascinate. He must take seriously the pleas of the world, which John Adcock has put in poetic phrases:

> We want no living Christ, whose truth intense
> Pretends to no belief in our pretense,
> And flashing on all folly and deceit,
> Would blast the world to ashes at our feet.
> We do but ask to see
> No more of him below than is displayed
> In the dead plaything our own hands have made
> To lull our fears and comfort us in loss—
> The wooden Christ upon a wooden cross.

Is this the indictment of our failure? Have we preached a Christ with no more relevance than some carved-out replica upon the wall?

If our preaching is biblical only in the sense that we string together a long list of proof-text Scriptures, never letting the thrust, the vitality, and the meaning of the Word push its way into the spiritual entrails of contemporary humanity—then we are not really preaching. If we spend our time debating theological controversies that are foreign to our people and their needs, fighting battles that ended long ago, setting up straw men upon which to launch our loud and gallant charges, then we are not preaching. If we spend our time spinning intricate answers to questions nobody is asking, while the pulse and heartbeat of existence pass us by and the open sores of suffering and injustice lie all about us in our own communities, then we are not preaching.

All about us life and experience—reality in depth—cry out to us. The people to whom we minister are not set apart from life; they are part and parcel of it. The dilemmas of existence are posed to people every day. Preaching is not designed to be a vacation from reality but a confrontation with life. Today's individual lives in a world that largely denies the reality of sin and evil but struggles nevertheless to find forgiveness, which exalts the preeminence of the material but longs nevertheless for a taste of the eternal. People today need anchors that will give life stability and purpose. They need assurance that they are individuals with basic and inherent importance, rather than minor cogs in a giant technological machine. They need guidance to know how to live with their neighbors, how to shed deeply-felt prejudices and hatred, how to give and receive love. They need to know why it's right to be honest and why it's good to be pure. They need to know what we really mean when we circulate the well-worn currency of the faith. What is repentance? What does it mean to believe, to trust, to commit? How can a dead Jesus become a living Christ of personal experience? In this ragged, frightened world, is God still in control? Where is God, anyway? Is God dead—or alive?

To be afraid to deal honestly and openly with these questions is to be afraid to preach. Preaching is God's answer through us to the needs of people. It must therefore take off the wraps and come to grips, both with the world we live in and with the people who live in that world.

Of course, some people will not like such preaching. Many people would prefer not to be disturbed by either truth or reality, if at all possible. Individuals

called to preach ought to decide very early whether they are volunteering for a popularity poll or a pilgrimage. The gospel is strong medicine for a sick world, and a good doctor never decides whether to prescribe a healing dose based on whether the patient likes the taste. "Mind your own business. Stick to the Bible," the world says. Preachers who are worth their salt will do exactly that. When they open the Bible, they read again the words of Amos, Hosea, Jeremiah, and of our Lord. They discover anew that the world's business is our business—every part of life.

"Go . . . preach," the Master said. Preach the word—not part of it, not just the soothing, pleasant part with which all people agree—but all of it. Preach the gospel—not the gospel divorced from life and experience, but the gospel that embraces all of life and pushes its way boldly into every phase of humanity's existence. Preach to the people—not to imaginary "religious" people segregated from reality for an hour on Sunday morning, but to real people with real problems. Never lower your standard of truth and righteousness, but build bridges by your preaching between that standard and the needs of men and women, so that they may see and understand that the gospel speaks to them.

One final word of admonition. With all that we have said about preaching, let us never forget that preaching is not something done by a man or woman in a pulpit to a group of people in the pews. Preaching—real preaching—is a holy experience of worship in which a spokesperson for God and the people to whom he or she speaks are caught up by the spirit of Christ. Preaching is something pastor and people do together. Preachers cannot speak only to the people; they must speak also to themselves. Thus, they must speak in humility, in fear and trembling, sometimes even from the depths of their own despair, but always with their faith centered on God in Jesus Christ. Preachers do not simply proclaim, "Thus sayeth the Lord." They weep with the people in their sense of common sin, and they rejoice with congregations in their gratitude for a common redemption.

This is preaching. This, I believe, is a little of what our Lord meant when he said, "Go . . . preach." When we obey that command out of hearts and minds and bodies committed to the full gospel of full redemption, the world may listen once again to what we have to say.

Note

1 Walter Lippmann, *Drift and Mastery* (New York: Henry Holt, 1914), 155-56.

6

A Small, Kind Word for JFK

(This article was first published in Christian Ethics Today.*)*

In the past few years, America and the world have been deluged with articles, books, and television documentaries revealing the alleged sordid details of the private and especially sexual life of former president John F. Kennedy. Indulging in a current popular blood sport, the media has pulled no punches in its pursuit of scandal—some of it quite possibly true, but some of it undoubtedly based on malicious hearsay and self-serving assumption.

I have read and watched this material with mixed emotions. I have no defense to offer for Kennedy's moral failures, but I must admit to being depressed by the whole sorry spectacle. I find it sad to watch the image of a former American hero being gleefully destroyed. After his tragic assassination in Dallas, Kennedy was elevated by the American public and the world at large almost to the position of a martyred saint. It was perhaps inevitable that his feet of clay should be laid painfully bare.

As a perhaps irrelevant interjection here, I would predict that much the same fate awaits someone like Princess Diana, whose unexpected death produced unnatural paroxysms of grief in Britain and indeed almost everywhere. Once the sensation-seeking journalists and revisionist historians do their work, the Princess will not fare well. She too had feet of clay.

In this connection, several observers of the modern scene have pointed out the disturbing fact that today we have few, if any, heroes—role models, objects of genuine veneration and admiration. I confess that once John Kennedy was one of my

heroes, based on what I understood of his political stance and compassion for the little man. I have now lost my hero and find that substantially more painful than losing something like a mere appendix. The world is a bleaker place without heroes.

As I write here in England, a continuing television series called "Heroes" is in progress on the BBC. A distinguished journalist, writer, and former Member of Parliament, Brian Walden, is each week giving a thirty-minute lecture on heroic figures of the past. Thus far, he has dealt with Winston Churchill and Abraham Lincoln. His intention is, he says, to consider such figures in total, "warts and all." Unfortunately, he spends almost all of his time dealing with the "warts." Neither Churchill nor Lincoln emerges from Walden's scathing scrutiny with much honor. I find his muckraking a thoroughly depressing spectacle.

As a Christian, I am constrained by all this to go back to the New Testament and the teachings of my Master. Years ago, a dear friend of mine, now dead, took up his first pastorate in an East Texas Baptist church. As he began his sermon on his first Sunday morning, he placed a rough piece of rock on the front of the pulpit, reminding his congregation of the words of Jesus as he knelt beside the prostrate form of a wretched woman taken in adultery. "Let him who is without sin cast the first stone." I list that statement among a number of the teachings of Jesus that most of us find difficult either to explain fully or to obey.

Perhaps my friend's gesture is a bit too dramatic for most of us, but there is hard truth behind the gesture. Jesus certainly condemned sin, including sexual sin, wherever he found it, but he never rejoiced in it. In the Kennedy affair I have been repelled by the eager interest of much of the public in every prurient detail of the story and especially by the unholy joy of some, openly exulting in the downfall of an American idol. The moral weakness and turpitude of another human being, however exalted his position, is not a valid source of amusement or delight.

Every moral condemnation that issued from the lips of Jesus was interlaced with profound compassion. He knew and taught that all people are sinners, each in his or her own way. No one human being's transgressions and weaknesses are carbon copies of someone else's moral failings. We each sin in our own way, and all sins are abhorrent in the sight of God. Few, if any, of us would relish the prospect of the public revelation of every detail of our private lives, especially those incidents

and episodes we have diligently sought to forget. It ill behooves us to gloat over the public moral nudity of someone else.

Just as important, I think, is that we remember that no human being is totally bad. We are all intricate mixtures of faith and doubt, selfishness and altruism, love and lust. Which is precisely why all of us—the John Kennedys and the John and Jane Does—must finally rely on the immeasurable grace of a loving God.

All of this reflection has led me to remember one small incident in my personal life, an incident that involved President Kennedy. Totally unimportant in the larger scheme of things, it is for me, nevertheless, a poignant memory.

The 1960 presidential campaign between Kennedy and Richard Nixon was bitterly fought, nowhere more so than in Texas, where I was a pastor at the time. In our area the campaign steadily degenerated in tone and spirit. In spite of the many real and important differences of policy and qualification between the two candidates, the major debate came to center on whether Kennedy, by upbringing and practice a Roman Catholic Christian, should be elected president. Platforms and pulpits reverberated to the claims of the prophets of doom. A dread picture was painted: if Kennedy were elected, the White House would be the servant of the Papacy and national policy would be dictated from some secret room in the Roman Vatican.

Political feeling was intense in the city where I served as a pastor. I did not believe then, and I do not believe now, that it is the responsibility of a minister to tell the congregation how to vote in a partisan political election. And as a practical matter, when I stepped into the pulpit on Sunday morning I faced in the pews one faithful deacon who was chairman of the county Democratic organization and another equally faithful deacon who was chairman of the county Republican party. I certainly had no desire to be involved in any sort of political controversy.

Then something significant happened. The pastor of the most influential Baptist church in the city decided to use his pulpit on a Sunday morning in early October to mount an openly partisan attack on Senator Kennedy. His tirade was based entirely on the fact that Kennedy was a Roman Catholic, and he used as his primary piece of evidence the so-called "Knights of Columbus Oath," which supposedly bound the members of that Catholic men's organization to a bloody persecution of all Protestants.

I knew—and I could not believe that my seminary-educated colleague did not know—that the "Oath" had over and over again been discredited and proved fraudulent by scholars of all faiths and of none. I also knew that there was no evidence that Kennedy subscribed to any of the beliefs set forth in that forgery. I was appalled and dismayed. There seemed to be no ethical or Christian justification for my fellow pastor's action.

The attack on Kennedy was picked up by the local press and then by state and national newspapers. It received headline attention. Though I felt strongly about the whole matter, my response as a careful man (which I believed myself to be) was strictly limited. I regularly wrote a column titled "From the Pastor's Study" for our church newspaper, distributed only to the members of our congregation. I used that column the following week to set out what I titled "A Call for Free Play." I detailed the indisputable evidence for the fraudulent nature of the so-called "Oath," and I urged my people to make their own decisions as to how to vote, based on the important and certainly debatable political issues.

I did not foresee the results. In the same way that the press seized upon the original attack, they now exploited my strictly church-related remarks. Headlines appeared in the local paper, and national press organizations gave the story wide coverage.

It was, as I remember, a Tuesday afternoon in late October of that year. I was beavering away in the church office when my secretary burst in, obviously in a state of high excitement. "Pastor," she almost shouted, "Hyannis Port, Massachusetts, is on the telephone. Senator Kennedy wants to speak to you."

I thought my usually calm and efficient secretary has suddenly had an attack of unexplained intellectual vertigo. But I must admit that I too was excited. It is not every day that a minor Baptist preacher gets a telephone call from a man who might well become President of the United States. When I picked up the phone, an anonymous voice insured that I was the proper person to take the call. And then there was the unmistakable, clipped, New England accent of John Kennedy.

"Mr. Wellborn," he said. "Forgive me for interrupting your busy schedule." (My busy schedule!) "I wondered if I could take a moment of your time." ("Yes, Senator, I think I can spare a moment.") "I want to tell you that we have gotten the press releases on your recent statement calling for fair play in the campaign. After what we've been getting recently in Texas, your remarks were like an oasis in

the desert. Let me assure you that we will make no use of your statement in our campaign. I have just called to express in all sincerity my respect and gratitude."

That was it—two minutes at the most. He did not ask me for any further statement or action. He did not even ask me to vote for him. He simply said in a gracious and, it seemed to me, sincere way, "Thank you."

So what, you may well say. It was an insignificant incident. And you are probably right, but forgive me if I wonder just a bit. I do not claim in any way to understand John F. Kennedy. I am no hypnotized Kennedy-ite, longing for a Camelot that never really existed. I am hard-nosed enough to believe that with high office comes increased responsibility, in both public and private areas of life. But when I view all the dark and sordid stories about Kennedy, I feel compelled to mix in one little moment, more than forty years ago—one simple, undemanding "Thank you."

No one of us understands completely the totality of another human being, even those we love most or who love us. There is something unfathomable to human intelligence about the human soul. Every little human entity is one of the enigmas of the universe, which is one reason why the scientists will never completely dissect us under the microscope or in the laboratory. And that is why one of the "blessed assurances" of the Christian is the faith that the God who stands both behind and in the universe and who has called each one of us into being does know and understand.

The New Testament tells the story of Zacchaeus, a miserable little man, who one day climbed a sycamore tree in his curiosity to catch a glimpse of Jesus. Beneath the tree Jesus stopped, looked up at that nondescript human specimen, and called him by name. Not only did he name him, but he insisted that he must go home with him. Jesus knew Zacchaeus and understood him in all his misery and littleness, just as God knows us all.

I remember one brief moment when John Kennedy and I made personal contact, but I share more than that moment with him. We share our humanness. My path has been different from his, and my weaknesses are peculiar to me, but we have both, I am certain, walked through the same valleys of moral ambiguity and ethical weakness. We professional ethicists, among whom I classify myself, work diligently to set out standards, rules, regulations, and guidelines for individual and

social behavior. In the final analysis, however, we are all human, and we fight a common battle.

That, I suppose, is why I feel constrained by my Christian conscience to say this one small, kind word for John Fitzgerald Kennedy.

7

BRANN VS. THE BAPTISTS: VIOLENCE IN SOUTHERN RELIGION

(This article was first published in Christian Ethics Today.*)*

Mainstream Southern religion has rarely been distinguished by either restraint or lethargy. Historically Southerners have, at least partly, agreed with Augustus Longstreet's "honest Georgian" who preferred "his whiskey straight and his politics and religion red hot."[1]

The result has often been scenes of conflict, usually verbal but sometimes violent, within the ranks of the predominant southern religious groups. The current arguments dividing Southern Baptists are but the latest in a long series of disputes going back in history to the days before the Civil War, when southern Baptists split with their northern brethren, largely over the issue of slavery. In the 1920s, amid controversy similar in some respects to the present situation, several leading professors at Southern Baptist seminaries were driven from their posts and went to other institutions, just as many teachers have been forced to do today. Such internecine struggles have often amazed outside observers. The Scopes "monkey trial" in Tennessee and the flamboyant antics of the Reverend J. Frank Norris[2] in Texas strike many people as exaggerated, overly dramatic, and soggily emotional. Yet to dismiss such personalities and events as mere aberrations in the history of Southern religion is unjustified. They are indicative, albeit in a grotesque way, of the deep roots of "Bible Belt" religion in the American frontier culture.

The emergence of the American South as the "Bible Belt" was profoundly shaped by the unique experiences of the early nineteenth century Second Awakening camp meetings in

Kentucky and surrounding areas. The revivalistic style of Christian conversion, set out as the norm in those meetings, both posited and demanded a decisive and virtually instantaneous separation of the converted person from the secular, non-Christian, Satan-dominated "world." In the frontier atmosphere of the camp meetings this separation was sometimes validated by distinctive emotional and physical manifestations (the notorious "jerks") and always by a deep-seated hostility toward certain selected and easily identifiable aspects of the "world"—liquor, gambling, dancing, and the theater, for instance. This hostility was not one-sided. Secularists, along with representatives of more genteel religious movements, found the Southern revival experiences distasteful and disturbing. Denominational groups such as Presbyterians and Episcopalians refused to participate, but other groups, particularly Baptists, Methodists, and Disciples of Christ, benefited enormously in terms of numbers from the meetings. And the gap between "Bible belt" religion and its detractors sometimes, and not unexpectedly, was bridged with violence.

In the last decade of the nineteenth century, William Cowper Brann, self-styled the "Iconoclast," indulged in a series of hotheaded assaults upon a large and influential segment of Southern Protestantism. He attacked Texas Baptists and their most important educational institution, Baylor University. His story offers not only a fascinating vignette of Southern religious history but also a case study in the violent working out of the hostility between church and world.

Born in rural Illinois, Brann spent most of his adult life as an itinerant journalist. At the age of thirty-nine he settled in Waco, Texas, which became the headquarters for a new magazine, *The Iconoclast*. This journal, a monthly compendium of personal philosophy, invective, and current comment, rapidly achieved an amazing degree of national and even international popularity. By 1895 Brann could describe his publication as "the first American magazine that ever secured 100,000 readers in a single year."[3] The staple ingredients in The Iconoclast menu, as the title indicates, were unrestrained attacks upon the central ideals and institutions of the contemporary political, social, and religious scene. Brann called his journal an "intellectual cocktail," and his verbal and journalistic talents served up a heady brew.

Waco, where Brann first came as an editorial writer for one of the local newspapers, was incongruously known both as the "Athens of Texas" and "Six Shooter Depot." Both slogans could to some extent be justified. The sixth largest city in

Texas at that time, Waco was the home of four important educational institutions. They were Waco Female Academy (Methodist), Catholic Academy of the Sacred Heart, Paul Quinn University (African Methodist), and Baylor University (Baptist). Of these the largest and best known—indeed, the pride of Texas Baptists—was Baylor, headed since 1851 by Rufus Burleson, a Baptist minister widely respected in Southern religious circles.

And, like ancient Athens as described by the Apostle Paul in Acts 17, Waco could be perceived as filled with people who were "very religious." Indeed, from the 1930s until after World War II, another popular sobriquet for Waco was "one tall building surrounded by Baptists."[4] No skyscraper marked Waco's skyline in Brann's day, but the city of 25,000 contained more than fifty churches, most of them Baptist with a sprinkling of Methodists, Presbyterians, Episcopals, and Catholics. Four monthly religious pamphlets, three of them Baptist, were regularly published in Waco.

Coupled uncomfortably with the educational and religious image of Waco was its reputation as "Six Shooter Depot," a hard-drinking, fast-living frontier community, many of whose citizens wore guns regularly in daily life. Shooting deaths were not uncommon, and in the 1880s Waco shared an unusual distinction with only one other American city—Omaha, Nebraska. A city ordinance set aside certain downtown blocks, known as the "Reservation," where prostitution and associated activities went on virtually unmolested by the city police.

Into this volatile civic atmosphere Brann tossed the explosive contents of *The Iconoclast*. He not only embraced unpopular religious and political beliefs; he also knew that controversy sells magazines. Where there was a divisive issue to exploit, Brann did not hesitate.

The long and bitter conflict between Brann and Waco's religious forces centered on a number of issues. One of Brann's favorite targets was the organization called the American Protective Association (A.P.A.), which exploited Protestant-Catholic tensions. Organized in the early 1890s in Canton, Ohio, the A.P.A. was not only anti-Catholic but anti-Semitic and anti-immigrant. It flourished briefly on the American scene and then disappeared. The A.P.A. sponsored traveling lecturers, some of them ex-Catholic priests, to espouse its cause. In April 1895, Joseph Slattery, ex-priest and recently ordained Baptist minister, gave a series of lectures in Waco, heavily attended and financially supported by the local Protestant majority,

especially Baptists. His most flamboyant effort was a "For Men Only" lecture on the evening of April 25. In a previous talk Slattery had made a long list of accusations against the Roman Catholic Church, outlining the so-called "Romish conspiracy" and including the claim that he had personally seen a true copy of a papal bull calling for a Protestant massacre in the United States "on or about the Feast of St. Ignatius in the Year of our Lord, 1893." He did not explain why the massacre had failed to take place.[5]

Word had spread in Waco that Brann planned to make an appearance at the Opera House where Slattery was speaking. The editor of *The Iconoclast* had already directed his attention to Slattery. In an edition of the magazine published earlier in April, he had written:

> Ex-priest Slattery and his ex-nun wife are still at large in the land, pandering to anti-Catholic prejudice and collecting money of cranks. . . . With some hundreds of Protestant preachers in the penitentiaries— and as many of their female parishioners branded as bawds—it were indeed remarkable if all priests were paragons of purity; but Slattery's sweeping denunciations would be promptly punished by due process of law did Catholic prelates consider him worthy of their serious consideration.[6]

Slattery had promised to reveal shocking and secret Catholic practices, too dissolute to discuss in mixed company, to his male audience. In the midst of his lecture, he deviated to attack Brann.

> He is simply a pipsqueak scrivener who has soiled your city with a calumnious rag called *The Iconoclast*, a fetid tangle of lies and half-truths, hiding his slander behind altars and anti-Christ slogans.[7]

Brann was indeed present in the hall. In the midst of the applause that followed Slattery's diatribe Brann rose to his feet, waited for silence, and then responded, "You lie and you know it, and I refuse to listen to you." He then walked leisurely to the door of the Opera House where, according to newspaper accounts of the incident, he blew a contemptuous kiss to the lecturer and left.

Later, Brann hired the Opera House at his own expense and delivered a public lecture replying to Slattery. His opening remarks set the tone of the controversy:

> *The Iconoclast* does not please ex-priest Slattery, "Baptist minister in good standing," and I am not surprised. Its mission, as its name implies, is to expose frauds and abolish fakes, to make unrelenting war upon Humbugs and Hypocrites; hence it is not remarkable that Slattery should regard its existence as a personal affront. It is ever the galled jade that winces; or to borrow from the elegant pulpit vernacular of the Rev. Sam Jones, "it's the hit dog that yelps."[8]

Brann included another shot at Slattery and his supporters in the May 1895 issue of *The Iconoclast*.

> Ex-priest Slattery and his ex-nun wife swooped down upon Waco recently and scooped in several hundred scudi from prurient worldlings and half-baked Protestants. . . . Brother Fight-the-Good Fight was out in force, and many a Baptist dollar went into the coffers of these brazen adventurers. . . . The audiences were representative of that class of so-called Christians which believes that everyone outside its foolish sectarian fold will go to hell in a hemlock coffin.[9]

In subsequent issues of his journal Brann continued to berate the A.P.A., which he dubbed the "Aggregation of Pusillanimous Asses," and the Baptist establishment. He branded the nationally known Baptist minister, T. Dewitt Talmadge, whose columns were carried in 3000 American newspapers, a "wide-lipped blatherskite." In an article that reveals Brann's own racial prejudices, he objected to the zealous foreign mission efforts of Baptists, while at the same time criticizing the wealth of the churches.

> For a specimen of audacity that must amaze Deity, commend me to a crowd of pharisaical plutocrats, piously offering in a hundred thousand dollar church prayers to Him who had not where to lay His head; who pay a preacher $15,000 per annum to point the way to Paradise, while

children must steal or starve. . . . Everywhere the widow is battling with want, while these Pharisees send Bibles and blankets, salvation and missionary soup to a job-lot of niggers, whose souls aren't worth a soumarkee in blocks of five. . . . Let the heathen rage; we've got our hands full at home. I'd rather see the whole black and tan aggregation short on Bibles than one white child crying for bread.[10]

In another issue of *The Iconoclast* Brann turned his caustic sarcasm on the influential monthly publication, the *Baptist Standard* (still today the official journal of Texas Baptists), edited by J. B. Cranfill, a Baptist patriarch. His special target was the advertising featured in *Standard* pages.

It grieves me to note that the purveyors of "panaceas" for private diseases regard the religious press as the best possible medium for reaching prospective patrons. . . . It shocks my sense of proprieties to see a great religious journal . . . like the *Texas Baptist Standard* flaunting in the middle of a page of jejune prattle anent the Holy Spirit, a big display ad for the "French Nerve Pill"—guaranteed to restallionize old roues.[11]

The event, however, that was to bring Brann's feud with the Baptists to a raging boiling point was one that shocked and intrigued all Waco. In spring 1895 the impending motherhood of an unmarried Baylor student from Brazil, Antonia Teixeira, became public knowledge. Antonia had come to Texas from Brazil at the age of twelve, sent there by Baptist missionaries to be educated at Baylor. During her first year at Baylor she was a boarding student on the campus, but then Dr. Burleson, Baylor's president, took her into his home where, in return for her board, room, and clothes, she assisted Mrs. Burleson with the housework.

Rooming in a house in the Burleson yard and eating his meals with the family was Steen Morris, the brother of Dr. Burleson's son-in-law. Morris worked for his brother, who published a Baptist monthly, *The Guardian*. According to Antonia, Morris sexually attacked her on three occasions, after first drugging her. She further asserted that she had reported the first incident to Mrs. Burleson, but that when Morris denied the story, no one believed her. Thereafter, she remained silent.

In April 1895, it was discovered that Antonia was pregnant. On June 16 the *Waco Morning News* reported the story in detail, including interviews with the Brazilian girl, Steen Morris, and Dr. Burleson. Morris was arrested on a charge of rape and released on bond, protesting his total innocence. Dr. Burleson denied that his wife had ever been told of any trouble between Antonia and Morris and labeled the idea of rape as preposterous. He declared that Antonia was "utterly untrustworthy . . . and in addition to other faults, the girl was crazy after boys."[12] A daughter was born to Antonia on June 18, but the baby soon died.

The situation was made to order for Brann, who saw the whole affair as a sordid scandal encompassing all the hypocrisy of the Baptists. In the July 1895 *Iconoclast* he set in motion events that were to lead to the deaths of four men. He wrote:

> Once or twice in a decade a case arises so horrible in conception, so iniquitous in outline, so damnable in detail that it were impossible to altogether ignore it. Such a case has just come to light, involving Baylor University, that bulwark of the Baptist Church.

Brann went on to attack Burleson for using the Brazilian girl as a "scullion maid" in the "kitchen curriculum," instead of giving her an honest education. With regard to her pregnancy, Brann asked rhetorically:

> What did the aged president of Baylor, that sanctum sanctorum of the Baptist church, do about it? Did he assist in bringing to justice the man who had dared invade the sanctity of his household . . . ? Not exactly. He rushed into print with a statement to the effect that the child was a thief and "crazy after the boys."[13]

Attacks on Burleson were inflammatory enough, but Brann compounded his offense in the eyes of Baptists with a general denunciation of Baylor. "I do know," he wrote, "that Antonia is not the first young girl to be sent from Baylor in disgrace—that she is not the first to complain of assault within its sanctified walls." And he concluded with a dramatic prediction:

> I do know that as far as Baylor University is concerned the day of its destiny is over and the star of its fate hath declined; that the brutal treatment the Brazilian girl received at its hands will pass into history as the colossal crime of the age, and that generations yet to be will couple its name with curses.[14]

As usual, Brann wrote in hyperbole. His prediction has not come true. But in 1895 his intemperate barbs aroused the resentment of every Baylor and Baptist partisan. Dr. Burleson, after conferring with his Board of Trustees, issued a four-page pamphlet titled "Baylor and the Brazilian Girl," in which he defended the university's role in the affair. The controversy continued for months, with Brann making new charges and rehearsing old ones in each succeeding issue of *The Iconoclast*. Morris's rape trial was delayed until June 1896, resulting finally in a hung jury, seven of the jurors voting for conviction, the other five for acquittal. In September 1896, Antonia Teixeira executed an affidavit exonerating Morris of her charges, then quickly returned to Brazil. Brann, predictably, asserted that the girl had been paid to sign the affidavit:

> When Capt. Blair (Morris's attorney) asks the court to dismiss the case . . . let him be required to state why the drawer of the remarkable document purchased Antonia's ticket, and who furnished the funds. Of course, her long conference with Steen Morris and his attorney on the day before her departure may have been merely a social visit. If the currency question was discussed at all, it may have been from a purely theoretical standpoint.[15]

In the year that followed the dismissal of the Morris indictment Brann continued to raise questions in print about Baylor and the Baptists. He ridiculed a plan, proposed in the *Baptist Standard,* that Waco Baptists should buy only from Baptist merchants. He attacked Waco's Sunday "blue laws," mocking the preoccupation of Baptists with Sabbath sales while they winked at the Reservation and the city slums. Again and again, he recalled Antonia Teixeira, whose "diploma" from Baylor was a dead illegitimate child.

A new dimension of the controversy emerged in October 1897. Dr. Burleson was about to retire from the Baylor presidency, and a political struggle to succeed him arose between B. H. Carroll, chairman of the university's Board of Trustees, and other aspirants for the office. Brann commented:

> I greatly regret that my Baptist brethren . . . should have gotten into a spiteful and un-Christian snarl over so pitiful a thing as Baylor's $2000 a year presidency—that they should give to the world such a flagrant imitation of a lot of cut-throat degenerates out for the long green.[16]

Evidently these new thrusts were the final straw for some Baylorites. On October 2 Brann was forcibly abducted by a group of Baylor undergraduates and taken to the campus. Had not several Baylor professors intervened, a lynching might have occurred. After being badly beaten the editor was finally released, but the violence was not ended. Four days later Brann was attacked by a Baylor student, George Scarborough, aided by his father, a distinguished Waco attorney. Young Scarborough threatened Brann with a revolver while his father beat the journalist with a cane. A second Baylor student joined the fray, striking Brann with a horsewhip. Brann fled for his life, escaping this time with a broken wrist, along with cuts and bruises.

The chain of violence was not fully forged. After an initial public scuffle between them had inflamed tempers, Judge George Gerald, a friend and supporter of Brann, and W. A. Harris, the editor of the *Waco Times-Herald,* met on a downtown Waco street. Present also was J. W. Harris, an insurance salesman and the editor's brother. Shots were fired; both of the Harris brothers were killed, and Judge Gerald was wounded.

The final act in the mounting tragedy occurred on April 1, 1898. Brann was to leave the following day on a nation-wide lecture tour. In the late afternoon he went downtown. From the door of a real estate office an anti-Brann zealot, Tom Davis, shot at Brann. Wounded, Brann drew his own pistol, returning the fire. Within hours both men were dead. Two bystanders were slightly wounded.

Why did Davis shoot Brann? His motives were not clear. He had a daughter attending Baylor, and he had expressed his hatred of Brann on many occasions.

He was also thought to have political ambitions, counting on his attack on Brann to win for him the sizable Baptist vote.

With Brann dead *The Iconoclast* soon ceased publication, and his feud with Baylor and the Baptists gradually faded into obscurity. Brann's career, however, is an interesting sidelight in Southern religious and political history. The ethical demands of Southern frontier religion did not prevent its adherents from violent reactions to Brann's attacks. It is perhaps significant that the thrust of those attacks was not primarily theological, though Brann was clearly a religious heretic in Baptist eyes.[17] Instead, Brann picked on at least three areas of special sensitivity in nineteenth-century Southern Protestantism: the conviction that "foreign" Roman Catholicism represented a major threat to the society and its values; pride in a major educational institution; and Southern sexual mores, a mixture of Puritan conviction and what Brann saw as Victorian hypocrisy. The bloody outcome of the struggle may testify to the underlying violent elements in both emotional Southern religion and the contemporary frontier culture. The reservoir of violence implicit in the intense emotional and even physical experiences of frontier revivalism was usually held in check by the ethical demands of the faith. The revivalistic conversion experience most often produced a constructive change in behavior and attitude, but it is not difficult to see how that violence could, under the proper circumstances and without the creation of great feelings of personal guilt, erupt in destructive ways.

A study of Brann's work reveals him as a master of brilliant and usually alliterative invective. He was a kind of provincial Voltaire who did not care if he sometimes twisted the truth so long as his efforts were directed against the "enemy" and brought him notoriety and profit. The affair of the Brazilian girl would probably have been quickly forgotten had not Brann nagged at it. Though it is impossible, after more than a century, to determine all the facts of the case with certainty, it is clear that Brann had some basis for his criticism, but it is also clear that he often tarred both innocent and guilty with the same brush. Brann's great talent was an unerring instinct for the vulnerable spots. He consistently went for the jugular vein. In retrospect, given the religious and social context, Brann's violent end seems almost inevitable.

Are there any lasting lessons from this small historical vignette? Perhaps we should reflect on the reality that, because religious experience and commitment

involve every part of the human psyche, they carry with them both constructive and destructive potential. The frontier culture of nineteenth-century Waco has largely passed away, and in today' s world, the potentially violent elements in religious faith most often, at least in America, find expression in verbal attack, bitter argument, and vitriolic abuse, rather than in physical violence. But we must not forget that in other parts of the world—in Northern Ireland, Bosnia, Kosova, and the Middle East—deep-seated religious differences are still capable of producing tragic human consequences.

Brann was buried in Oakwood Cemetery in Waco, and a monument capped with a Grecian urn inscribed "Truth" was erected at his grave by his friends. Carved into the stone was a profile mask of the dead writer. Scarcely had the monument been erected when someone, under the cover of darkness, crept into the cemetery and fired a pistol shot at the stone memorial, shattering away a portion of the mask. The scar in the stone can still be seen, a vivid reminder of the passions inspired by the "Iconoclast."

Notes

1 Quoted in Winthrop S. Hudson, *Religion in America* (New York: Charles Scribner's Sons, 1965), 137.

2 Norris was pastor of the First Baptist Church, Fort Worth, Texas, from 1909 until his death in 1952. During his turbulent career he was accused of burning down his church auditorium to collect the insurance. He also shot a man in his church office but was acquitted of a charge of murder on a plea of self-defense.

3 Charles Carver, *Brann and the Iconoclast* (Austin: University of Texas Press, 1957), 71. Carver's volume is the fullest available study of Brann.

4 The "one tall building" was the headquarters of the Amicable Life Insurance Company, erected in the early 1930s.

5 See Carver, *Brann and the Iconoclast,* 8.

6 *The Iconoclast* 5/3 (April 1895).

7 Carver, p. 14

8 *The Complete Works of Brann the Iconoclast,* vol. 12 (New York: The Brann Publishers Inc., 1898), 204-205. See also Carver, *Brann and the Iconoclast,* 14-16. Carver's account of the incident differs from the account given here. Carver describes Brann as engaging in a long debate with Slattery in the Opera House. The description given here, taken from the collected edition of Brann's works, is probably more accurate.

9 *The Iconoclast* 5/4 (May 1895).

10 Ibid. (May 1895).

11 *The Iconoclast* 5/2 (March 1895).

12 *Waco Morning News* (16 June 1895): 5.

13 *The Iconoclast* 5/6 (July 1895).

14 *The Iconoclast* 6/8 (September 1896).

15 *The Iconoclast* 7/9 (October 1896).

16 *The Iconoclast* 8/10 (1897).

17 Brann consistently denied that he was an atheist. In the March 1896 issue of *The Iconoclast* he wrote, "There is a Deity. I have felt his presence. I have heard his voice. I have been cradled in his Imperial robe. . . . I ask no written covenant with God, for he is my Father. I will trust him without requiring priests or prophets to indorse his note."

II

8

REFLECTIONS OF A SOMEWHAT DISILLUSIONED "PROPHET"

(This article was originally published in Christian Ethics Today.*)*

This is a purely personal reflection. In the title, the word "prophet" is in quotes. In no way would I claim to be an Amos or a Joel or seek to classify myself among authentic modern Christian prophets such as Martin Luther King Jr., Will Campbell, or Carlyle Marney. I am a minor player in the league.

My only claim to the title of prophet arises from the fact that from my first day as a Christian (and I was already an adult), I nourished a then inchoate assumption that an essential part of the Christian minister's job description was the role of prophet—not as a foreseer of the future, but as a thoughtful Christian critic of the present. My initial understanding of the task of the prophet has remained with me through the years.

I became a Christian at the age of twenty-three in the remarkable southern youth revivals of the 1940s. Already scarred by the unmentionable horrors of war service, I found my personal answers in a traumatic and emotional conversion experience. After more than fifty years I do not question the reality of that experience, but it was a conversion brought about by an encounter with the Christ-event, not a conversion to any human institution, creed, or organizational statement of faith. And that is important.

Less than five years after I became a Christian, following seminary study and a short spell of teaching, I was called to the pastorate of Seventh and James Baptist Church, located virtually on the campus of Baylor University, Waco, Texas. I accepted that call. In many ways it was a ridiculous decision, both for me

and for the church. The church was a large one with a long and honorable history. Gifted men like Jeff Ray, W. W. Melton, and Woodson Armes had been among its previous pastors. I had never been a pastor, and I knew almost nothing about the mechanics of church administration. One thing I thought I did know: part of my job as a pastor was to try to be a prophet.

So it was that within three months of assuming the pastorate I preached a series of Sunday evening sermons on "The Christian and Contemporary Issues." I tried as best I could to bring the ethical demands of the Christ-event to bear upon race, war, economics, and the family. When I read those sermons now, I readily see how inadequate and immature they were, but at least I was trying. And I kept on trying. As an eager young pastor, I did not spare the horses. I was reckless, sometimes radical, often extreme. And, to be honest, I gloried in it. There was a sort of wild exhilaration in preaching the whole truth as I saw it, however unpleasant that truth might be. No diminution in the evangelistic thrust of the pulpit took place, but the prophetic note was sounded again and again.

Here I must say a word of gratitude to the patient congregation of Seventh and James Church. They listened tolerantly—more than that—to my rantings and ravings. I cannot judge how much some of them may have been honestly influenced by my sermons, but never once in my ten years as pastor did a member of my congregation advise me to "tone it down."

Race was the overwhelming ethical issue of the 1950s. Both I and the church came finally to take our stand on the issue. In 1958, with few dissenting votes, the church officially declared itself to be an "open" church, with no barriers to membership on the basis of race or color. The results were not dramatic. We did not have, as some of our people had suggested, a flood of new black members. In fact, for a long time, we had none. We lost only a few of our membership in protest. The most obvious result came in the somewhat pathetic outbursts of the local racial bigots—obscene midnight telephone calls, a crude cross burned in the front yard of the parsonage, one wall of the church sanctuary defiled with lewd graffiti. These events allowed me to exult in the role of a bit of a martyr, but I was not mature enough to realize the insidious temptation of spiritual pride that confronts all self-styled martyrs.

The church did well. Our membership steadily increased to the point that we were being tagged as the largest Protestant university church in the country.

We baptized more than a hundred converts in most years. We built a new sanctuary seating more than 1200 people and attracted around 2000 worshipers to two Sunday morning worship services. In the process I was learning and maturing. Increasingly, however, I became convinced that my ultimate role in the ministry was not as a pastor but as a teacher.

In 1961 in a chain of events that seemed to me almost miraculous, developments opened a practical financial way for me to pursue further education as preparation for teaching. With a wife and two children I left, with great affection, Seventh and James, and began doctoral studies at Duke University.

The next few years were times of difficulty and personal tragedy. For a variety of reasons—some of them my responsibility, some not—my marriage failed. In the Southern Baptist world of that day that marked the end of any effective preaching or teaching ministry within the ranks of my denomination. Fortunately I found my niche at Florida State University, first as Chaplain to the University, then as a professor of religion, and finally as dean or director of the university's overseas campus in London, England, where I remained for almost twenty years until my retirement. The career opportunities that my own denomination could not afford me, a secular university did.

My excuse for this extended personal history is that my present understanding of the prophetic task is rooted in and has been shaped by my experience, and I cannot ignore it. Throughout the years I have continued to preach, though not normally in Baptist pulpits. I have never lost my conviction as to the role of the preacher as prophet. My Christian faith is as strong as ever. And, in spite of everything, I am still a Baptist by conviction.

In the fifty-five years since my ordination as a Christian minister, what have I learned about prophecy? Why do I class myself as "somewhat disillusioned"? I believe it is because I have had to face what I call "the parameters of prophecy."

First, it is relatively easy to be prophets so long as we confine ourselves to generalities and choose our issues carefully. Almost everyone, as Calvin Coolidge (and others) said, is against sin. When pastors, especially in more conservative pulpits, thunder in general terms against liquor, gambling, abortion, adultery, homosexuality, or prostitution, they can count on a chorus of "amens," especially from the choir. They may even reap tolerant and somewhat bemused approval from those

members of the congregation who themselves drink, gamble, or even commit adultery, since that moral stance is the widely accepted public one in church circles.

The difficulty comes when preachers begin to take seriously the complexities of these moral problems. Does the angry denunciation of abortion take into account the genuine tragic dilemma of a pregnant teenager facing choices that include a loveless marriage or bringing into the world an unwanted but innocent child with limited chance of ever reaching social or psychological health and maturity? Does a ringing condemnation of homosexuality deal with any degree of compassion with the real problems of those luckless individuals who, as a result of either heredity or environment, have never had a genuine chance to work out their own sexuality? I use only these two examples. There are many more.

Once one gets beyond the "safe" issues, the prophetic road becomes a rocky one. How do preachers deal with the complexities of an increasingly greed-oriented, "me-first" economic system? Market economy and free enterprise ride triumphant in today's world, even in crime- and corruption-ridden Russia, but the gap between the nation's—and the world's—haves and have-nots grows steadily wider. Feast and famine dwell side by side in the earth's richest societies.

And what of race? Most of the legal barriers in our country have gone, and we can rejoice in that. But the hard core of personal prejudice is still with us. How do prophets deal with that? And what of the thorny issues of affirmative action and race quotas, where the positive and negative arguments often seem almost equally convincing?

I could expand these areas endlessly. The basic thing is this: prophets have comfortable ground on which to stand only so long as they deal in generalities and confine themselves to carefully chosen issues. Quite naturally, a cafeteria-like approach to issues is the popular road.

A second parameter is this: Christian prophets are far better at denunciation than at constructive solutions. In my later theological education I was exposed to thinkers like Reinhold Niebuhr who taught us that politics is "the art of compromise." Positive compromise, yes, but nevertheless compromise. Crusades for the absolute ethic are seldom effective in changing the secular world. In that world almost all choices are, to be trite, not between white and black but between shades of gray. Black and white are the normal color spectrum of the Christian world, but gray is the prevailing shade in the secular arena. One valuable lesson of history is

that moral revolutions, like political ones, in the name of a flaming absolute often produce as much chaos and human suffering as the evils that have been destroyed in the process. Politically, the French and Russian revolutions are cases in point. On the social and moral level one can look at the "Great Experiment" of Prohibition and the resulting gangsterism, political corruption, and contempt for law that followed.

Christians must constantly participate as good citizens in political campaigns and elections. How do prophets deal with these concrete and essential mechanisms of government? The hard fact is that, when I go to cast my ballot, I never have a clear choice between a saint and a sinner but rather between two or more sinners of varying hue. The current attitude of cynicism about all politicians is no excuse for nonparticipation. Christian citizens are doomed to leave the polling place with a rueful sigh, knowing that, at best, they have chosen the lesser of two evils. They have been forced to compromise.

In the secular world, compromise is almost always the only road to progress. Prophets are faced with holding at one and the same time two conflicting stances. They must continue to proclaim the judgment of perfect Christian love upon the world while at the same time giving impetus and support to those gradual, unsatisfying, and imperfect political and social steps that may improve the real situation, at least a bit. It is a knife edge, and no easy escape is available. If prophets do their job conscientiously, they are almost certainly doomed to cries of dissatisfaction and resentment from many quarters.

The third and final parameter is this: the hard fact of universal sin. I am not theologically a Calvinist. I cannot live with the cold and heartless logic of Geneva. But through the years I have been forced to deal with the realities of what the Calvinists call original sin and total depravity. I have my own understanding of these doctrines. I do not believe that a just God ever punishes any of us because of the sins of our ancestors, though their sins, like ours, always have consequences for the innocent. I do not believe than any person is totally evil. But I cannot help discerning what someone has called the "greasy thumbprint" of sin in everything that I and others do.

In this regard the stance of prophets is problematical, for they are always and everywhere sinners speaking to other sinners. The most subtle of temptations for prophets, caught up in the exhilaration of condemning the evil in others and in

society, is to forget, at least for the moment, the evil in themselves. We are all without exception participants in humanity's sin, not simply observers and critics of it. I often wonder how seriously most Christians take the confession of the Apostle Paul when he declares, "I am the chief of sinners." Was that simply literary hyperbole or did the Apostle actually mean it? And if he meant it, what of us?

I have said that the temptations to prophets in this area are subtle. Perhaps nowhere can this be seen more clearly than in what we call "the power of the pulpit." Preachers have the totally legitimate mission of proclamation and persuasion. Where do we draw the line between this legitimate task and the crude but skillful use of rhetorical devices to override the free wills and minds of the congregation? I dare say that most honest preachers would admit that they have sometimes felt the satisfying surge of personal power that comes when they realize that they hold their listeners in the palm of their hand. True, the Holy Spirit works in mysterious ways. But if clever oratory, personal charisma, or simple bombast bring members of an audience to the place where pure emotion overrides the sober intellect or a form of mild hysteria infects a congregation, have we not in some measure failed to rely on the Holy Spirit? Is this not a clear mark of that "greasy thumbprint"? And if, as a preacher, I glory in it, am I not then "chief of sinners"?

Power is, of course, a key word here. The lust for power is a vital and universal ingredient in the human psyche. It creeps in insidiously everywhere. Many of us have watched with growing pain the internecine squabbles of Southern Baptists over the past few years. I have, metaphorically, squirmed in my pew as I have listened to leaders on both sides of the conflict descend to character assassination, personal diatribe, and pious shibboleths. I have suffered by proxy with the countless good men and women whose lives have been crippled, maimed, and destroyed. And I venture to say sadly that almost any objective observer would agree that what we have seen has not really been any great crusade for doctrinal purity or creedal conformity but a squalid struggle for power and control—the "greasy thumbprint."

Do the combatants in this supposedly titanic struggle ever listen to the lessons of history or the teachings of their own ancestors in the faith? Or do they only respond to the all-too-human dictates of original sin and total depravity? Do they ever remind themselves that the greatest of their human patron founders—

Roger Williams—always fighting against creedal conformity, died, not as a creedal Baptist, but as a self-styled "seeker after truth"?

The lust for power is the most deadly, along with sexual lust, of human temptations. To ignore it, especially in oneself, is the road to hypocrisy, self-delusion, and uncompassionate self-righteousness.

So I am "somewhat disillusioned." I am not disillusioned about the prime necessity of the prophetic task, but I have come to recognize some of the magnitude and difficulty of that task. Preachers must be prophets. There is no escape. But preachers must recognize the realistic parameters of their mission, and, above all, they must approach that task with deep humility and a sense of their own inadequacy. Only God's grace can empower that mission, and God deals, I believe, most generously and gracefully with those who come to God in earnest consciousness of their own sin. Perhaps it helps to remember that one of the true heroes of the faith is that man in the New Testament who responded to the Christ, simply and honestly: " Lord, I believe. Help thou my unbelief." The strange mixture of faith and unfaith is a reality in all our lives.

God is the only true and final judge of human affairs. God through Christ gives us the "living water." Preachers are called to be dispensers of that water, but the water is always channeled through rusty pipes. In a world of ethical ambiguity and prophetic uncertainty, prophets must strive, ever conscious of their limits, to point men and women to the final imperative of perfect love.

9

IS IT MURDER? THE PROBLEM OF
ETHICAL LANGUAGE

(This article first appeared in Christian Ethics Today.*)*

One of the most distinctive attributes of the human race, setting men and women apart from any other species, is the power of verbal communication. While some experiments have seemed to show evidence of rudimentary communication among animals such as chimpanzees by means of signs and grunts, and while some people have fantastic theories about dolphins, the human ability to communicate not only simple facts but complex ideas remains unique. Human language is still, in many ways, a puzzling mystery to psychologists, neurologists, and linguists.

While human verbal and written communication is a highly developed and distinctive skill, it is not without problems. Sir Francis Bacon, the sixteenth century lawyer and philosopher (who some people believe wrote Shakespeare's plays), recognized those problems when he wrote in his influential treatise, *The Advancement of Learning,* "The first great judgment of God upon the ambition of man was the confusion of tongues; whereby open trade and intercourse of learning was chiefly embarred."

While one might quibble with Sir Francis as to whether, scripturally, this was the first judgment of God on a sinful human race, he stands on solid ground in terms of the Old Testament story of the tower of Babel, which tells us that God punished the pride and ambition of the people by "confounding" their language. The story is often employed as an explanation of the myriad of different human tongues—English, Chinese, Arabic, etc. But it can equally well

apply to the manifest ambiguities and difficulties of interpretation within a single language, such as our own English.

Many of the words we use in everyday verbal intercourse can communicate different understandings. Take the word "love." When someone says to you, "I love you," what does he or she mean? The word may convey simple lust, mindless obsession, passionate regard, deep affection, the desire for manipulative possession or jealous ownership, friendship, altruistic concern—the list of meanings can go on and on. The interpretation of those words by the one to whom they are addressed is conditioned by many factors: knowledge of the speaker, the context in which the words are spoken, and, perhaps in many cases most importantly, by what in a particular set of circumstances he or she wants the words to mean.

H. Richard Niebuhr, the American theologian, pointed out that the process of communication is not complete until what he called "the gesture"—the initial words or action—is interpreted and responded to by the recipient of that gesture. The interpretation of the meaning of any individual gesture and the consequent reaction to it are always shaped and bound by the unique physical, intellectual, emotional, and cultural situation. There is insight in the pronouncement of Humpty Dumpty in Lewis Carroll's *Alice through the Looking Glass*: "When I use a word, it means just what I choose it to mean—neither more nor less."

These observations have a particular relevance to the problem of how Christians are to understand the words of the Scriptures. The Bible is given to us in human language, words set once and for all in a particular format. Those Christians who believe in what is called "verbal inspiration"—that is, the idea that each scriptural word is in the fullest sense directly inspired by God, overriding any personal beliefs, characteristics, or limitations of the human writer—must deal seriously with a basic question. If this understanding is a true one, how are the inspired words then to be interpreted? Since many words are susceptible to a variety of interpreted meanings, the thoroughgoing verbal inspirationist can never stop with mere words. He must specify, among all the choices, the precise meaning of the inspired word. This means that he must devise creeds, catechisms, and dogmas to specify the exact and "correct" meaning of the words. What is obvious through twenty centuries of Christian history is that preachers, theologians, and the rank and file of Christian believers have arrived at many different understandings of the meaning of the same sets of biblical words. When some Christians begin to try to

enforce their particular interpretations on others, or to maintain that they and they alone have understood the only correct meaning of the words, they are claiming for their human views the same divine imprimatur as the Scriptures themselves. This seems to me, as one sinful human being among many, an impossible position. I cannot accept that any individual, group or human organization can lay claim to such infallible divine authority.

In the realm of Christian ethics, a case in point is the interpretation of the meaning of the Decalogue. Christians accept the Ten Commandments as a solid, God-given basis for healthy moral conduct. But what do the words of the commandments actually mean, when applied in actual life situations?

Take, for example, the sixth commandment, "Thou shalt not kill," more accurately translated as "You shall do no murder." The commandment clearly places an extremely high value on every individual human life. To bring any life to an untimely end is a serious matter. "Murder" can be defined as unjustified killing. Here, the application of the moral law takes on complexity. What actual circumstances "justify" the taking of human life? The answer to that question has been the subject of debate and disagreement through the centuries. Christians have looked at such issues as the killing of enemies by soldiers in wartime, capital punishment, abortion, euthanasia, birth control, and actions in self-defense, all of which arguably involve the taking of life or the prevention of its development, and have reached widely different conclusions.

Across the centuries one can discern an irregular pattern of development in the understanding of the meaning of "murder." In ancient times a widely held view was that the prohibition of killing applied only to family and clan members. Thus, the killing of Abel by Cain was essentially the crime of fratricide. Gradually the meaning of "murder" came to include the killing of members of one's own tribe, and then, of members of one's own nation. Christian pacifists and conscientious objectors argue today that the killing of any human being, even in war, is sinful and unjustified. The problem in this regard has been heightened by the slaughter of civilians and noncombatants, including women and children, in modern "total war."

Clearly, the understanding of the meaning of the sixth commandment has been materially shaped by the contemporary cultural context. At this point Christians need to be especially careful in their approach to the interpretation of the Hebrew Scriptures. Numerous sections of the Old Testament present genuine

problems of ethical understanding. We believe that the Old Testament is given to us by God as an instrument of edification and the understanding of spiritual truth. It tells the story of the struggle of Israel to understand and obey God' s law—and, indeed, the struggle of God to convey God's will to them. That struggle was replete on Israel's side, as the Hebrew prophets repeatedly pointed out, with human misunderstanding and error. Again and again Israel misconceived or twisted the concept of a loving God. We are to learn and profit by not only the valid insights gained by Israel, but by their mistakes.

Two examples out of many will help make the difficulty plain. We are told in the book of Joshua that when Jericho was conquered, the Israelites, in obedience to Joshua's command, "utterly destroyed all that were in the city, both men and women, young and old, and ox, and sheep, and ass, with the edge of the sword" (Josh 6:21). Are we to believe that it was actually the will of a loving God that innocent women, children, and even animals should be brutally and cruelly put to the sword? Or is it more sensible and consistent to believe that Joshua, a sinful man and, to some extent, a prisoner of his culture, misinterpreted God's will in a spirit of vengeance? Christians must always view the Old Testament through the eyes of Jesus. Is it possible for us to imagine Jesus sanctioning such a massacre? Were the lives of the inhabitants of Jericho worthless in the sight of God? Was the killing of Jericho's women and children "murder"?

The book of Judges relates one of the more tragic stories in the Old Testament. Jephthah, military leader of Israel, preparing for battle, tries to bargain with God and makes the foolish vow that if God grants him victory, he will sacrifice whatever first greets him when he returns home. Victory is achieved, and when Jephthah arrives home, he is greeted first by his only child, a daughter. In fulfillment of his vow, he sends his innocent daughter to her death.

What are we to make of this? Are we to see it, as preachers sometimes extol it, as a great act of faith and obedience on the part of Jephthah? Or are we to see it as the disastrous story of a sinful man, misunderstanding the will and character of God, committing "murder"?

Perhaps I can press the point with a far-fetched, hypothetical modern example. If President George H. Bush, at the beginning of the Gulf War, had publicly vowed that, if God gave America victory over Saddam Hussein, he would sacrifice whatever first met him at the White House door, how would sensible people,

including Christians, have reacted? And if the President had been greeted on his return by his eldest son, George W. Bush, and in fulfillment of his vow had sent his son to his death, what would have been our judgment on him? The whole example is, of course, ridiculous, but the fact that we cannot conceive such a scenario surely passes some sort of judgment on Jephthah.

Concrete examples of the shaping of the interpretation of the Scriptures by culture can be multiplied almost endlessly. In the sixth century, Procopius, secret court historian for the Emperor Justinian in Constantinople, wrote of his Christian master (who had built the magnificent Santa Sophia and left his enduring legacy with the Justinian legal code), "He did not accept that the crime of murder extended to those who did not agree with him on theological or, indeed, other matters. He slew them without compunctions of conscience." In the Middle Ages the leaders of the Holy Inquisition piously believe that it was the will of God for them to torture or even kill in order to preserve the purity of their doctrine. In the years leading up to the American Civil War devout pastors across the South proclaimed that the Scriptures endorsed and approved the institution of human slavery, surely a kind of extended "murder" of body and spirit. Today, few, if any, honest Christians would support these interpretations of God's moral law. We easily recognize that such distortions of biblical teaching resulted largely from cultural conditioning. It is more difficult for us to accept that our own understandings may be similarly flawed.

To return to Richard Niebuhr's terminology, the Scriptures can be seen as a "divine gesture." That gesture is communicated to us through a particular set of words. The process of communication is not complete until we interpret and respond to the gesture. Our response, as sinful people locked up in a time-space box that conditions our every thought and action, is always and everywhere partial and problematical.

I have concentrated here on one particular biblical injunction: "You shall do no murder." I have emphasized the difficulties of interpretation when we apply the moral law to specific problem areas. I have deliberately not set out my own views on such issues as war service, capital punishment, abortion, and euthanasia. I certainly have views on each of these problems, and I am prepared to argue my views in the appropriate forum. But what I want to make clear here is that my views on these issues are personal ones, and I claim no pseudo-papal infallibility for them.

Our responses must take account of the complex dimensions of the problems. Look at the issue of capital punishment, for instance. Is legalized killing by the state the "justified" taking of human life? The answer to that question cannot be given by a simple repetition of the Scriptural text. True, the Old Testament routinely, in accord with its cultural context, seems to approve forms of capital punishment, often in cruel and barbarous forms. And the New Testament nowhere specifically condemns capital punishment as such. (It should be remembered that the New Testament is also silent on many other issues that were not relevant to the time in which it was written but that are modern moral problems, such as the exploitation of children or environmental pollution.)

Today's Christian approach to the morality of capital punishment must take into account any number of questions, some of them factual and others ethical or philosophical. What is the acceptable purpose of capital punishment? Obviously, it is not reform or rehabilitation of the condemned person. Is it a deterrent to the commission of other capital crimes? If it is, would it not be more effective to follow the example of previous societies and use the most painful and public methods, such as open-air hangings or the guillotine? It is taken for granted that any legal process should involve justice. Are we certain that the legal bureaucracy we have set up to make decisions on capital punishment is a fair and equitable one? Is it worth the risk for society to execute ten guilty murderers if it also executes one innocent person, caught up in a fallible system? Does legalized execution ultimately humanize or brutalize the total society? If the punishment should fit the crime, which is worse—a quick, "humane" execution, or to be locked away for years in the "hell-holes" that modern society calls prisons? Is the economic factor decisive; that is, the comparison of cost between executing a criminal or imprisoning him or her for long periods of time? Should legal justice strive to be totally objective, or should it be influenced by the understandable emotional demands for revenge on the part of the victim's family? Does final judgment involving the death of a human being belong to the state, or should final judgment be left to God?

I suggest that these questions only begin to reveal the complexity of the issue. My rhetoric may at times betray my personal view, but my view is not the core of the problem. We are seeking the best moral truth we can find.

Where does all of this leave us? Is there hope for progress in our understanding of God's "gesture"? I do not think that any progress will arise out of dogmatic,

creedal pronouncements, whether those dicta originate in Rome, Nashville, or Salt Lake City. Our hope now, as in the past, rests in a continuing, open dialogue within society and within the Christian community. What is essential is free, untrammeled discussion and debate among those who honestly seek moral enlightenment. That dialogue must be firmly set within the real-life parameters of the twenty-first century. It must take into account all the valid dimensions of the problem. But there is still new light to burst forth from the old Book.

In the process we must not be afraid to take hard new looks at old problems. There is no change in the original words of the Scriptures, but there is continuing change in human interpretations of that Scripture. My own Baptist forebears— people like Roger Williams and John Leland—were branded heretics by the established religious authorities of their day. If history has taught us anything, it is that yesterday's heresy is often today's orthodoxy. New light does come, but it comes only through the free dialogue of committed Christian believers armed with honesty and humility. Human declarations involving claims to some sort of divine infallibility are often the last resort of those who find it difficult or impossible to defend their views within the wider Christian family.

There is no escaping our Christian responsibility. God has given us the Scriptures as well as minds and spirits. I believe we are expected to use those gifts in the continuing search for God's will in matters of moral conduct. The job is tough, but "toughness" is one appropriate description of the Christian life. Given our human limitations, the answers at which we arrive may rarely be final or definitive, but the quest must continue.

If the Christian family is what it proclaims itself to be—a "community of love"—we must make certain that changing and differing understandings of biblical language must not be allowed to shatter the bonds of Christian fellowship. While holding strongly to our own honest perceptions, we must not allow our differences to sever us from other Christians who have just as honestly arrived at different perceptions. We are all engaged in the same search. We must always be ready to listen to what others believe and to enter into a meaningful dialogue with them. It is only in this way that we can hope for any real moral progress. We might even come to a clearer understanding of what the sixth commandment means when it says, "Thou shalt not kill."

10

LAW AND LOVE: DOING THE ETHICAL DANCE

(This article first appeared in Christian Ethics Today.*)*

Years ago my friend Herbert Blomberg, a Jewish rabbi, told me a fascinating story out of his people's history. Some medieval Jewish congregations in Eastern Europe once practiced an unusual form of worship. At one point in the service the rabbi would lift the Torah, the symbol of the sacred Law, from its resting place and, holding it high above his head, would dance. His movements were traditional and strictly prescribed. The dance was always performed in exactly the same way. When the rabbi had finished this section of the service, he would replace the Torah in its accustomed place. Moving to another lower section of the synagogue, he would again begin to dance. This time, however, the dance was different. No longer prescribed or planned, it was a spontaneous, improvised series of movements—a dance of freedom.

As I reflect on this story, I am reminded of certain features of modern popular music and dance. As a university administrator for many years, part of my responsibility has involved attendance at student dances and discos. As I have listened to the music and watched the couples on the dance floor, I have often been visited by a wave of nostalgia—a symptom no doubt of age. I long for the music of my youth: big bands, tuneful melodies, and the sentimental rhyming lyrics of "Stardust" and "Deep Purple." Today's popular music often seems to have no discernible melodic line, and the words are frequently crude, banal, and repetitive. What matters almost exclusively is the "beat," a rhythmic pulsation that dominates the music. I have sometimes been kept awake late at night by the excessively

loud music played by my student next-door neighbors. What penetrated the walls of my bedroom was not a melody or a lyric but a pounding "beat."

Modern dance displays similar characteristics. The popular dances of my younger days were waltzes, fox-trots, two-steps. A prescribed pattern dictated the movements in each dance. I seem to remember that the once ubiquitous Arthur Murray dance studios had footprints painted on the floor to aid beginners in making the exact steps. In today's dancing, by contrast, few of the movements are prescribed. The dancers rarely touch each other. Each person dances individually, freely, spontaneously, improvising as he or she goes. One restriction remains. The dancers must conform to the "beat," the underlying rhythm of the song being played.

In using these illustrations I am not ascribing undue significance to modern dance. How young people dance may have some importance for the students of popular culture, but that is not my concern. Rather I want to use these observations as metaphors for the Christian's obligation to act responsibly in demanding moral situations. In making moral choices all of us are frequently faced with the difficult task of balancing two essential standards—law and love. We are not free to ignore either of these standards. Our proper response in such situations is what I want to call "the ethical dance."

I have pointed out the dominant role of the "beat" in today's popular music. In my metaphor the "beat" represents the role of the moral law. I do not refer here to statutory or governmental law. That is human law, and human law is constantly changed, amended, or repealed. The divine law is always there, unchanging and implacable, etched in Old Testament terms in "tablets of stone." Thus, Jesus, as a legitimate bearer of the divine word and an incarnation of a new moral dispensation, never denied or ignored the law. Instead, he went beyond the law; he "fulfilled" it. His revolutionary moral stance involved a drastic reinterpretation of what it means to be "good" and, therefore, a radical reshaping of the law itself. He taught that the law must always and everywhere be seen and understood in the light of a new and far more demanding ethical standard, that of love. This is not to say that there was no love in the Hebrew Scriptures or in the Jewish handling of the law. But Jesus placed a special kind of love—what we have come to call agape, a totally unselfish and unmerited love—at the apex of the moral pyramid, over-shadowing all else. In honestly facing the moral requirements of the law as

88

redefined by love, those who are committed to the Christ are called to "dance"—
to work out in concrete real-life situations the often difficult moral equations
involving the "beat" of the law and the free spontaneity of love.

The essence of the law is most clearly spelled out for us in the Old Testament
Decalogue, the Ten Commandments. The Commandments are a terse distillation
of the fundamental moral perimeters of a humane and good society. God gave the
Commandments to Israel so that, by adherence to them, his people might be a
"holy nation," operating as a continuing moral example to the world around them.
But the Commandments cannot have been conceived as a comprehensive or
detailed guide for every moral action. They mark out areas of transgression and
moral obligation, but they do not address the intricacies that arise in actual human
conduct. They prohibit murder but do not spell out exactly what murder is. They
condemn "false witness" but give us no detailed explanation of such witness. God
left his people with the responsibility of interpreting the implications of his fundamental moral commands. Israel's attempt to fulfill that responsibility resulted in
the meticulous complexity of the Old Testament ceremonial and legal system.
Indeed the Old Testament delineation of the law essayed a finally impossible
task—to anticipate every possible moral situation and provide a clear and unar-
guable legal provision, leaving no room for human confusion or deviation.

The essence of the Commandments is as important for today's world as it was
for Israel. They define the moral limits of a functioning humane and godly society,
and any individual, community, or nation choosing to ignore those limits opts for
risk and ruin. Throw away the underlying structure of the law and the result will
be not just moral anarchy, but a total cultural collapse. I am no Chicken Little
trumpeting on flimsy evidence the news that the sky is falling, but I must admit to
a serious concern and disquiet about the well-being of our American society when
I see on television the devastating scenes of the Littleton, Colorado, school horror.
A parade of experts bemoans the event and asks over and over again, "Why?" No
one seems to have an answer, but a forthright and honest look at how far our society has drifted away from the moorings of the moral law might offer clues.

Be that as it may, it is important to remember that, basic as the
Commandments are, they are not God's final word in the moral realm. When
Jesus was asked, "What is the great commandment of the law?" he responded
without hesitation, "You shall love the Lord your God with all your heart and with

all your mind and with all your soul." But he did not stop there. He turned that commandment over like a coin and read the reverse side. "And the second is like it. You shall love your neighbor as yourself."

With those words Jesus clearly set out a new moral standard based on the ultimate supremacy of love. Moral obligation involves two dimensions of love—God-love and neighbor-love. The two loves are inseparable. In the final analysis, while we must listen to the "beat" of the law, the moral quality of any act or decision is measured by the dimensions of love. Thus, to live the good life requires the constant balancing of love and law. Such balancing calls for a careful interpretation of the meaning of the law in the light of love. It requires that the interpreter be constantly open to the freedom and spontaneity that must characterize agape as it is applied in real-life—not theoretical—situations. Such responses constitute the "ethical dance."

In the April 1999 issue of *Christian Ethics Today*, Gilbert C. Meilander, Jr. offered a persuasive argument against the Kantian concept that, for an act to be considered moral, it must stand the test of universalization; that is, a conception of what would happen if every person in a similar situation made precisely the same decision. He called attention to a complex range of personal decisions such as, for example, the choice of vocation, that do not lend themselves to that test. While making his point effectively, Professor Meilander also conceded that there are certain moral duties "which bind us all and which we are free to omit only at our moral peril." He goes on to give as examples of such inescapable duties those enjoined in the Decalogue.

Meilander's contribution is valuable in shedding light on the important differences that exist among various types of moral decisions and the consequent differences in how these decisions ought to be made. I do wish to raise a caveat, perhaps unfairly, since Meilander does not really address this particular issue. Like him, I have argued for the universal and unchanging nature of the basic moral law. But to acknowledge this is not in any sense to diminish or limit the individual's responsibility to give even these fundamental commandments a thorough bath in love. In making a decision in any concrete situation that involves these basic injunctions, the decision-maker faces two different responsibilities. He or she must say "yes" to the moral absolute of the commandment, but he or she must then go further. It is necessary to decide upon the precise human actions that are

compatible with that preliminary "yes." It is at this point, I believe, that love enters into the process. In the light of my "yes" to the commandment, what is my appropriate and loving action? I think I would argue more strongly than Meilander that agape—God-love and neighbor-love—must be brought to bear as the primary element in every moral decision, even those personal ones involving such things as vocational choice.

Perhaps an example will clarify what I am trying to say. In the previous essay, "Is It Murder? The Problem of Ethical Language," I pointed out that the sixth commandment clearly establishes the sanctity and value of each human life. It categorically forbids murder. I believe that every sincere Christian must say "yes" to that commandment. But the affirmation of the commandment as a moral absolute does not automatically solve many important moral problems. The Christian decision-maker is left with the responsibility of working out through the use of reason within the spiritual environment of the Christian community which human acts constitute "murder" and thus are forbidden by the commandment. Is, for instance, the killing of an enemy soldier in wartime an act of "murder"? There is no prepackaged or universally agreed on Christian answer to that question. The believer must find a personal answer.

A particularly painful example of this process is the vexing question of the morality of abortion. Is every abortion "murder" and therefore unequivocally forbidden by the sixth commandment? Many Christians think so. They take the position that inviolate life and personhood begins at the moment of conception. This is essentially, though not exclusively, the Roman Catholic position. If one believes this, and further believes that the preservation of the life of the fetus at any stage of its development takes moral precedence over all other considerations, it follows naturally that abortion is "murder." This is a fairly simple solution of a moral problem.

The fact is, however, that many sincere Christians emphatically do not agree with that interpretation. For one thing, they see the current state of scientific knowledge, so far as it related to the personhood of the fetus, as a mixed bag. For another, they view the fetus in terms of the development of personhood, rather than simply biologically. And for a third thing, they want to factor into any abortion decision what they consider to be other important concerns, such as the

freedom of a woman to control her own body and the future well-being of a child brought into the world irresponsibly.

I am not here concerned to take sides in this thorny issue. I am rather trying to illustrate two things: first, the moral responsibility of any Christian is not completed simply by saying "yes" to a general moral absolute, and second, the implication of that "yes" must be carefully worked out in a process undergirded by the primary role of God-love and neighbor-love.

In setting out this position I do not think I am departing from the teaching of the Scriptures. To do the "ethical dance" is an essential part of our humanness, a state of being that derives directly from our belief that we are created "in the image of God." The reflected God-image in humanity is a spiritual one, and a basic component of that image is the ability to make free choices. If we have no such freedom, we are less than human—part of the lower nonhuman orders of creation. Without moral freedom there can be no such thing as love, in the New Testament sense of the term, only instinctive feelings or simple lust. In the Genesis story Adam and Eve used their moral freedom to disobey God. Though saddened by that decision, God did not override it. God allowed the built-in consequences of that disobedience to operate. Adam and Eve were expelled from the garden. Guilt replaced innocence. The consequences of sin or wrong moral choice are written into the fabric of the disobedient act. But unless there is genuine possibility of wrong choice, there is no moral freedom and, therefore, no humanness.

Humanness involves much more than the free power to choose. God did not leave us without resources for making right choices. Our moral decisions are not simple "stabs in the dark." For one thing, God has given us the law, fulfilling the functions set out above. A second gift from God is the human ability to reason. Christians believe that the universe is one of order, a planned entity. Such a belief is not the simple-minded conviction that at any moment this is the best of all possible worlds. God's order is constantly being upset by our disobedience, but we believe that the patterns of the Divine Mind are reflected, albeit in a limited way, in the mind-patterns of human beings. The human power to reason is a gift of God and, therefore, a valuable resource for making proper moral decisions. If our logic and reason do not somehow reflect an ultimate reality, all human life is nothing more than a series of unrelated or accidental incidents, linked loosely by secondary causal factors but without any final meaning. Thus, to quote Shakespeare, "life is a

tale told by an idiot, full of sound and fury, signifying nothing." Of course, there are many people who deny any ultimate meaning to the universe, but it is paradoxical that these thinkers in reaching that conclusion are employing the method of reason. In other words, they are using human reason to deny any final universal reason, a logically flawed position.

Human reason, employed in the making of moral decisions, provides a tool by which we can attempt to measure the consequences of any action and include in the decision-making process as many relevant factors as possible. Reason also helps us to be aware of the limitations of our freedom. We are not free to do anything we want in a real-life decision-making situation. There are always circumstances that limit our available choices. "Politics," said Reinhold Niebuhr, "is the art of the possible." So too is moral decision-making. To some degree our scope of moral action is always limited by the circumstances. We can only do what we can do. Reason aids us in discerning those limits.

Reason alone, however, does not complete the picture of humanity created in the image of God. God has made us not only reasoning beings but spiritual ones with the capacity to relate to the Creator and to draw guidance from that source. This spiritual capacity allows us to realize that, in the area of moral choices, human reason is not sufficient. Pure reason can often lead to inhuman and unloving moral decisions. Even a carefully worked out logical concept such as Immanuel Kant's "categorical imperatives" can lead to profoundly destructive choices. The Jesus standard of love, brought to bear on the ethical process, will not permit, however "reasonable" the decision may appear to be, an action that is not coherent with the loving and redemptive purpose of God.

The use of reason alone, separated from the overriding standard of love, is the basic constituent of legalism in the worst sense of the word. Unless it is immersed in love, legalism by its very nature tends to degenerate into a set of impersonal abstractions. It is not difficult to see why legalism has always exercised a seductive appeal for many Christians. We hunger for a "simple" moral system—one that removes any doubt as to the "rightness" of our decisions and also relieves us of the responsibility of wrestling with complex and ambiguous situations. We must realize that this approach is a kind of ethical "cop-out." To surrender the love-motivated freedom and spontaneity of moral decision-making is to give up an essential element of what makes us fully human. Consistently applied legalism can reduce us to

moral automatons, left only with the minimal ability to say "yes" or "no" to a life-less, loveless verbalism.

The continuing difficulty of balancing law and love—doing the "ethical dance"—has dogged the Christian community from its beginnings. In the forma-tive stages of the New Testament church a crisis arose when the Apostle Paul was led to extend his preaching to the Gentile world. Paul understood the gospel to be of universal significance, speaking to the basic problems of every human being, whether "Jew or Greek, male or female, slave or free." His vision was crucial for the emergence of Christianity as a truly worldwide religion. Without that vision the Christian faith seemed destined to be only one among many Jewish sects. The decision of the early church is recorded in the chapter 15 of the book of Acts. James and the other leaders of the church at Jerusalem had previously insisted that a Gentile who became a Christian must also become a Jew (according to the law), subject to the ritual of circumcision and the full requirements of the Old Testament. Paul argued for the Christian faith as a radically new relationship between people and God, based not on ritual or moral legalism but on loving grace. Paul's understanding prevailed and, as a result, the gospel was set free from a legalistic straightjacket.

No sooner, however, had this basic problem been solved than an opposite cor-ruption of the gospel arose. Some Christians seized upon their freedom from legalism—the "curse" of the law—to posit and practice an alternative "easy" way out of the difficulty of making moral decisions, the heresy of antinomianism. If believers are no longer bound by the law and if grace is sufficient for the forgive-ness of every sin, why should they not disregard entirely the moral admonitions of the law? If where "sin abounds, grace does much more abound," why should Christians worry about sin at all? Why should the believer have to struggle with the complex dimensions of moral freedom?

The Apostle Paul saw antinomianism as a problem equally as serious as legal-ism. He responded by emphasizing the legitimate moral function of the law. The law, he argued, is primarily valuable to us because it reveals the true dimensions of sin, including wrong moral choice. Aware of these dimensions, the Christian must apply to his or her life the more stringent requirements of love. The believer does not live in an amoral world. Against the indispensable background of the law—the "beat"—he or she must do the "ethical dance." Paul insisted that there was no easy

way to be good. Goodness arises neither out of robot-like obedience to the letter of the law nor out of reckless, unprincipled disregard of the law. Moral decision-making is a difficult, even sometimes dangerous, endeavor, arising out of the spirit-led struggle of reasonable yet fallible human beings to act in love. The decisions made will not always be totally right; indeed, all decisions made by sinful humanity will be partial and flawed. This realization imposes upon us the virtue of humility and the necessity for open-mindedness. We are always open for correction.

For the Christian this is an inescapable responsibility. Seeking to live the God-loving and neighbor-loving life is an essential part of the process of Christian growth—the way in which we progress toward becoming the kind of human beings God purposes us to be. "Therefore, be mature, even as your Father in Heaven is mature," Paul counsels us in the Philippian letter. Becoming mature—perfect—is God's ultimate goal for creation.

My own judgment, open to legitimate argument, is that there are few honest Christians today who seriously adopt an antinomian position, at least in theory. Obviously, there are many people who live an antinomian lifestyle without trying to justify it with formal theology. But for many people who seriously want to be "good," legalism retains its allure. At this point it is salutary to recall that some of the harshest words of Jesus in the New Testament are reserved not for blatant sinners like Zacchaeus or the woman taken in adultery, but for those staunch defenders of adherence to every jot and tittle of the law, the Pharisees. These zealous law-keepers were Jesus' prime example of self-righteousness. Indeed, there is something endemic in legalism that pushes individuals toward self-righteousness. Checking off all the instances in which one has obeyed the law is conducive to spiritual pride and an exaggerated estimate of one's own goodness. It is often the self-righteousness legalist who ignores the admonition of Jesus to "judge not, lest you be judged." The Pharisees exemplified the working out of that admonition. Their proud assumption that they were qualified to serve as moral judges automatically put them on the receiving end of judgment.

In summary, what I have tried to say is that, for Christians to become what God intends for us to be—mature human beings made in God's image—the moral struggle is not an elective but a requirement. If we seek to shun that struggle or find an "easy" way out of it, we are guilty of moral cowardice. It is often our fear of making the wrong decision or our unwillingness to tackle difficult and complex

decisions that paralyze our capacity to love and block our progress toward Christian maturity. We possess the God-given freedom to choose among the available alternatives of action in any ethical situation, but with that freedom comes the responsibility to employ every means at our disposal to make the most loving decision. If we listen with honesty and humility to the "beat" of the law while never forgetting the overriding supremacy of love, I believe we can do the dance of responsible moral freedom. No one can live a Christian ethical lifestyle without learning this dance.

11

THE SHAPE OF JUSTICE

(This article first appeared in Christian Ethics Today.*)*

What is justice?

At first glance that appears to be a simple question. Many people would answer, "Justice is fairness," and be satisfied. Yet the distillation of the essence of justice and the perplexing problem of what constitutes "fairness" in real-life situations have occupied the attention of many of the world's best legal, philosophic, and religious minds for centuries. From Plato and Aristotle in the ancient Greek world through Thomas Aquinas in the medieval period to modern legal scholars such as John Rawls, the meaning of justice has been endlessly debated.

In the October 1999 issue of *Christian Ethics Today,* Ruth Ann Foster of Truett Seminary at Baylor University gave a perceptive delineation of "biblical justice." She rightly emphasized the partiality of that justice and its inherent bias toward the marginalized and oppressed individuals in society. The inbuilt final purpose of biblical justice is the redemption of human beings, body and soul. Forgiveness, mercy, and compassion are seen as powerful forces in the redemptive process.

An oft-used example of the workings of biblical justice is the familiar story of Jesus and the woman taken in adultery (John 8:1-11). The woman had committed a crime. Jesus did not condone or excuse her crime. Rather, he illustrated his trust in the power of redemptive love by forgiving the woman of her sin. With mercy and compassion he told her, "Go and sin no more." At the same time he focused attention on the hypocrisy of her accusers: "Let him who is

without sin cast the first stone." Many Christians have found in this story an insight into the core of the Christian gospel.

If we study this incident in the search for the full meaning of justice, however, we must remind ourselves of certain salient considerations. It is important, for instance, to note that Jesus was not operating within the precincts of a formal court of law. He was dealing with an individual in a one-to-one relationship, and he was free in that context to exercise forgiveness and mercy, unhindered by any statutory codes of jurisprudence. Clearly, the actions of Jesus in this particular case provide a valuable pattern for the personal and moral conduct of his followers. Compassion and its accompanying special concern for the downtrodden and oppressed in this world are essential elements in the Christian life. They are not options for the believer but ethical imperatives.

When we seek to translate these imperatives into real-life situations, however, we face major difficulties. In our society the Christian must be aware of two types of justice—biblical and legal. The distinction between the two is necessary and inescapable. In ordinary life people are constrained to operate within communities and under governments. This means that we are bound within the limits of statutory prescriptions, as enacted by legislatures and interpreted by courts of law. Quite clearly, biblical and legal justice are not one and the same thing. Thus, in this area as in many others, the Christian citizen faces the problem of how to "render unto Caesar that which is Caesar's, and unto God that which is God's."

In Professor Foster's article referred to above, she correctly rejects the traditional symbol of justice as a blindfolded woman with a pair of scales as an inadequate representation of biblical justice. Still, that figure is frequently used as a symbol of legal justice. The woman with her scales stands above the entrance to the Old Bailey, London's Central Court of Criminal Justice. It is possible to argue that, while inappropriate as a symbol of biblical justice, the figure is significant as a representation of impartiality, the keystone of legal justice.

When a Christian citizen sits as a judge or a member of a jury, he or she is subject not only to biblical imperatives but also to the complex demands of a statutory judicial system. Had Jesus been in such a position with the adulterous woman as an indicted prisoner before the courts, he would not have been free to say, "Go and sin no more." Legal justice, in contrast to biblical justice, does not—and cannot—operate in that fashion. It demands that all relevant facts be presented and a

decision made as to the guilt or innocence of the person on trial. If, in the type of case we are discussing, the jury finds the prisoner guilty, it is normally the responsibility of the judge to impose a sentence within certain strictly defined limits. In this situation the symbol of the blindfolded woman is entirely appropriate. Ideal legal justice is characterized by equality of treatment for all those who come in conflict with the law, regardless of such factors as race, gender, religion, or social and economic situations.

Does this emphasis upon the differences between biblical and legal justice mean that they are irreconcilable and that there are no relevant points of contact between the two? I think not.

When we recognize the partiality and special concern of biblical justice for the poor, it is necessary to remember certain important considerations. First, biblical justice neither condones nor overlooks the seriousness of criminal and unloving acts, whether these acts are committed by the rich and powerful or the poor and powerless. If a murder has been committed, for example, a human life—often a totally innocent one—has been tragically ended. The consequences for that individual and for his family and associates, all beloved by God, are inescapable. It is in this sense that the revolutionary and violent terrorist, however just he or she may feel their cause to be, cannot plead justification for destructive acts purely on the basis of poverty, oppression, or marginalization in society. Every human life is infinitely precious to God. Because all of us are individuals with a significant degree of free will and moral choice (though the scope of that freedom will vary from individual to individual), we all must necessarily face the consequences of our actions. The man or woman who commits a legal crime must be judged by legal justice if a community, state, or nation is to function at all.

The second thing to remember in this connection is that biblical justice does impinge in fundamental ways upon legal justice. Biblical justice demands that, within the operations of legal justice, every individual should be treated, not as an object or a "case," but as a valuable human being. The legal concept of "fairness"—equality before the law—is a reflection of an important essence of biblical justice. Insistence in legal practice upon the veracity and validity of evidence and the right of every accused individual to a speedy, orderly, and impartial judgment by his or her peers is certainly consistent with the structure of biblical justice. Furthermore, biblical justice insists that the state abstain from certain types of

"cruel and inhuman" punishment—torture, for instance. Biblical justice constantly seeks to inject into legal justice elements of humane and civilized behavior.

I want here, however, to go beyond this basic area of identification between biblical and legal justice to emphasize one particular way in which legal justice within its own structures can be shaped by the injunctions of biblical justice, with its special emphasis on attention to the poor and socially impoverished elements in our society, the so-called "shadow people."

In the early development of English law, the most important basis of the American legal system, the major constituent of jurisprudence was the "common law." In the absence of any substantial body of statutory legislation in medieval England, judicial decisions had to be based on and reflect the common customs of the society and community. Many cases were decided by reference to previous judgments. Out of these specific judgments grew general precedents that guided judges in particular cases. Subsequent cases, however, might reveal new and different circumstances for consideration. Many of these unique situations were the result of the constantly changing social and technological dimensions of the society. In such cases the common-law judge was free to depart from precedent and establish a new rule of decision, thus establishing a new precedent for other magistrates adjudicating in similar situations. In this way common law incorporated a dynamic for change. As Supreme Court Justice Oliver Wendell Holmes wrote in his treatise, *The Common Law* (1881), "The life of the common law has not been logic; it has been experience."

Alongside the common-law courts in medieval England, a parallel system of jurisprudence developed—courts of equity. At first, equity courts were administered by the Church, but gradually they became part of the state's legal structure. Equity courts originated in English law when subjects petitioned the monarch for relief in specific legal situations, especially those instances in which the common law did not seem to provide opportunities for justice. Equity developed into a special body of rules and judgments over and above those administered in other courts. Courts of equity provided legal remedies based on ideas of "fairness" to litigants or accused whose situations could not properly be judged by common law.

Over the centuries the development of extensive systems of specific legislation and judicial statutes took over most areas formerly covered by common law and equity, so that in modern times in both Britain and the United States statutory law

has come to encompass most legal situations. Both the common law and the concept of equity, however, remain important in the interpretation of statutory laws, many of which are restatements of common law and equity principles.

It seems to me that the precepts of legal equity provide a significant bridge between legal and biblical justice. In his influential book A *Theory of Justice* (1971), John Rawls, the contemporary legal philosopher, draws extensively on ethical considerations, primarily those involving equity, to support his understanding of the meaning of justice. He develops the proposition that no advantage for any one group in a pluralistic and diverse society has the moral right to exist, if that advantage does not in the long run benefit the most highly disadvantaged elements of that society. This implies that legal decisions should incorporate as an essential element a consideration of the relevant social, environmental, and economic circumstances of the accused or the litigants. Such an approach to legal justice certainly involves an application of the core of biblical justice, though Rawls himself does not explicitly spell out this connection. Whenever the important background factors are ignored, serious miscarriages of justice, especially from the biblical point of view, are all too likely to occur.

An over-simplified illustration may illuminate this point. Most people—certainly, most Christians—would agree that the transgression of a poor woman who steals a loaf of bread to feed her hungry family ought not to be judged on the same level as the crimes of an individual who, out of selfish greed, defrauds thousands of people of their life savings. True, both acts are thefts in statutory terms, but considerations of equity should certainly operate in the assessment of punishment or penalty. (As an aside to attorneys who may read this, I am not presuming to deal with specific legal aspects of equity but rather with a general concept.) While considerations of equity cannot override statutory specifics, the idea of "fairness" as a working legal principal is certainly necessary.

For the Christian citizen there is also another avenue of connection between legal and biblical justice. Statutory law is enacted by legislatures, setting up judicial procedures and penalties. In a democratic society the Christian citizen has the opportunity to be involved in the political process in which laws take shape. From a Christian standpoint legal statutes should, whenever possible, be influenced by biblical concepts such as the equality of all individuals before the law and the essential humaneness of judicial procedures and penalties. As an example, it is

certainly a Christian imperative to seek to emphasize in our penal system the necessity of rehabilitation—a concept sadly too often forgotten in our modern prisons, labeled by many experts as "universities of crime." And we can certainly question the fairness of the present system as it relates to the death penalty, too often obviously applied without proper regard to the personal situation or background of the condemned.

A sensational murder case in Britain can serve as a vivid illustration of what I am trying to emphasize here. I am quite sure that similar illustrations could be drawn from American legal history. In February 1993, two boys—Robert Thompson and Jon Venables, each aged ten years—enticed a two-year-old child, James Bulgar, away from a shopping mall where his mother lad left him unattended while she browsed in one of the mall's shops. The boys took the toddler with them to an isolated area near a railroad track and there, for reasons never adequately explained, killed the child. (It never became clear whether both boys or only one actually participated in the murder.) No apparent motive existed. James Bulgar was not sexually molested and had nothing of value for the boys to steal.

The horror of this brutal act and the lack of motivation made the crime one that could be easily sensationalized, and the press, especially those tabloids known in Britain as the "gutter press," took full advantage of the opportunity. By the time the two boys were arrested and charged with the crime, a climate of "mob justice" and "lynch law" had been created. The police, the courts, and politicians were all under tremendous public pressure. Even before the boys were tried and found guilty, editorials and screaming newspaper headlines were demanding vengeance in the name of the slain two-year-old and his distraught family.

In this atmosphere the events that occurred were not surprising. The two boys (by the time of the trial, one was eleven, the other still ten) were tried in what was essentially an adult court. They sat through complicated judicial procedures that were obviously beyond their comprehension. In the months before they were found guilty they were given psychiatric examinations but were denied treatment for what any objective observer could see were obviously disturbed personalities.

During the trial the presiding judge refused to allow any testimony regarding the home, social, or economic background of the two boys, ruling that such evidence was irrelevant and inadmissible. The only fundamental question raised was "Did the boys have any recognition of the fact that what they were doing was

wrong?" In fact, both children came from broken and impoverished homes and had been reared in an atmosphere of contempt for the police and the law. They were frequent school truants whose parents had made no serious attempt to keep them in school. The quality of whatever moral training the boys had received could be seriously questioned. None of these circumstances were allowed to influence the final verdict and sentencing.

The guilty verdict was reached after less than an hour of jury discussion. The trial judge then assessed what was in effect life sentences on both boys but fixed a minimum eight years of detention before they could be considered for any possible parole. Upon reviewing the verdict the Lord Chief Justice raised the minimum term to ten years. The press screamed its protest at the verdict, and the Home Secretary, who in Britain is the political head of the judicial system, genuflected to the popular outcry and overrode the judgment of the courts, raising the minimum period of imprisonment before possible parole to fifteen years.

Britain does not have capital punishment, but elements of the British people and press are continually calling for its return. They used the Bulgar case to reinforce their demands. By their standards the two boys would have been executed. For these people—who demand a wasted life in payment for a wasted life—the Bulgar case provided a powerful platform to shout for the blood of the two convicted children.

The case reemerged in the public consciousness in late 1999 when the Inspector of Her Majesty's Prisons, a highly respected public official, ventured the opinion, based on his study of the development of the two boys during their years of detention, that they might well be considered by the Home Secretary for an earlier parole hearing than had been previously prescribed. Both boys had been model prisoners and, in particular, Robert Thompson had made significant progress in his schooling and was preparing to take college entrance examinations, called "A" levels in Britain.

The outburst that followed this announcement was predictable. The Inspector was accused of being "soft" on crime and a "weak-kneed liberal." Understandably, James Bulgar's parents reacted with indignation. Less understandably, the "gutter" press screamed with horror and fury. The Home Secretary apparently put pressure on the Inspector, and he publicly retracted his statement.

One further development is significant. Early in 2000 the European Court of Human Rights, which within the structure of the European Community has jurisdiction over British courts in this type of case, ruled on an appeal of the now six-year-old verdict that the two boys had not received a fair trial, since the proceedings of an adult court would be intimidatory and incomprehensible to children of their age. The Court also specified that hearings in such cases should be held in private or at least with limited public and press attention. The Court further declared that purely political individuals, such as the Home Secretary, should not interfere in the legal process and that sentencing was a matter properly left to judge and jury. The Court's decision raised the possibility of a new trial for Robert Thompson and Jon Venables.

Are there important lessons to be learned from this sorry incident for the Christian citizen seeking to relate legal and biblical justice? I have highlighted this particular case, but I believe there are general lessons to be learned.

(1) At what age does a child become morally and, therefore, criminally responsible for his or her actions? A precise answer to this question is extraordinarily difficult, but any answer must certainly take into account individual differences. It is absurd to say that all children reach an equal age of accountability at a set calendar age. Social and environmental factors, as well as the quality of the moral training that the child has received, must be taken into consideration.

Virtually every reputable child psychologist would agree that children, in general, are less able than adults to realize the long-term consequences of their actions on other people, to reflect on their behavior, or to experience feelings of guilt and shame. These abilities develop as the child's personality develops and matures.

(2) I repeat here my conviction that neither legal nor biblical justice allows those who commit crimes such as murder to escape responsibility for their acts. The individual concerned is guilty and must be punished, and the public as a whole must be protected from such further acts on his or her part. But it must also be stressed that the type of punishment should be, certainly in terms of biblical justice, redemptive and rehabilitative. I submit that this concern is doubly important when the law deals with acts committed by children. While, ideally, all penal sanctions should carry the element of rehabilitation, the opportunities for such redemptive treatment are obviously much greater when we are dealing with very young offenders. It is, I believe, un-Christian to believe that a child's life is totally

ruined beyond repair, however terrible act he or she has committed. I know no Scripture that supports such an idea.

(3) At the very least, children should not be tried for offenses in an adult court setting. In Britain and, so far as I know, in the United States (though the exact age may differ), criminal offenders under the age of eighteen who are charged with less serious crimes are dealt with in youth or juvenile courts. Such practice implicitly recognizes the inappropriateness of adult courts for these individuals. Yet, in Britain when charged with murder or other more serious crimes, children must be tried in an adult setting. Following the tragic school shootings in the United States, some people have demanded that the culprits—none of them adults—should be handled as if they were fully responsible adult individuals. To accede to these demands seems to me to be little more than an illogical sop to an atavistic public.

To return to my general proposition, I have argued that biblical justice should not be confused with legal justice. The actions of Jesus in a one-to-one personal relationship outside a formal court of law cannot be simply and without modification transferred to the domain of legal justice, bound by statutory law and judicial precedents.

I have also argued, however, that there is a viable bridge between biblical and legal justice provided by judicial equity or "fairness" and that this bridge is a means of introducing the biblical demand for consideration of all relevant circumstances relating to a crime or to an accused criminal. In this way the Christian concern for the poor and oppressed becomes an important constituent of legal justice. Such an approach is consistent with the dimensions of biblical justice in real-life situations. It avoids a naive, oversimplified approach by Christians to complex problems. In this regard the oft-asked question "What would Jesus do?" is a legitimate one, but only if its application is fully understood.

I would suggest that in an increasingly complex society, the question might well be rephrased as "What could Jesus do in this actual situation (assuming that Jesus acts in his fully human capacity, as we mortals must act)?" Put in this way, the question recognizes the concrete and inescapable limits within which human beings must operate.

The common phrase "the art of the possible" applies to the total ethical and moral task of Christians in a modern world. This does not in any way constitute a

watering-down of the moral imperatives of Jesus or an abandonment of the ethical demands of the Christian faith. Rather, it opens up in practical ways the opportunity of Christian citizens to influence effectively the "shape of justice" in everyday life.

12

RADICAL SOUL LIBERTY: OUR FUNDAMENTAL NATURAL RIGHT

(The following is a slightly expanded version of a statement made to the Conference on Religious Liberty convened in London, England, in July 1999. The conference was sponsored by the Cooperative Baptist Fellowship, the Baptist Joint Committee on Public Affairs, and the Baptist Union of Great Britain.)

The title of our session is "Challenges to Mere Toleration." The title is a pejorative one, chosen by someone with definite convictions about the meaning of religious liberty. The term "mere toleration" raises immediate questions about the adequacy of that concept.

Let me position myself. I am a practicing Christian and have been for more than half a century. My conversion to the Christian faith came when I was a World War II veteran, newly discharged from combat service, and my commitment to my faith is rooted in a deeply personal spiritual experience that I cannot with any integrity deny or compromise. Secondly, I am a Baptist Christian by tradition and conviction. A fundamental part of my Baptist stance is an adherence to the doctrines of the priesthood of the believer, the primacy of the authority of personal religious experience, the separation of church and state, and radical soul liberty. I identify with historical figures such as John Bunyan, Roger Williams, and John Leland, all of whom risked their lives in defense of religious freedom.

Against that background the concept of religious toleration satisfies neither my spiritual nor intellectual conscience. As a case in point, I use the British situation since we are meeting here in London. I am an expatriate American who has lived in Britain for more than twenty years because of vocational commitments.

I confess that never in that time have I experienced any practical limitation of my religious freedom. But I am a professional political ethicist and the theory of an established church with close links to the state disturbs me. I agree with the Anglican Bishop of Woolwich who wrote, "The church of God must be free. . . . The church must in conscience take responsibility for its own life, rather than having its constitution, faith, rules, and appointments in the grip of others."

I would only add to the Bishop's statement that not only his own church, the Church of England, much of which I admire and respect, but every other church, religious group, and, indeed, every single individual is entitled to that same freedom.

Toleration is an offensive word to me because it necessarily implies that one established group has the right and power to grant others the right to differ. If an authority has the right to grant toleration, it also has the power, at least in theory, to withdraw that toleration.

In actual practice, despite that underlying theory, British law often acts effectively to protect the religious rights of the individual. A recent minor incident vividly illustrates that point. A fundamentalist Christian preacher chose the front steps of an Anglican cathedral as his pulpit. There was no service being conducted in the church. The doors of the church were closed. The church authorities ordered him to leave. He refused. He was arrested for a breach of the peace. When he appeared before the local magistrate, he was immediately freed. The judge said in his statement, "Whatever an individual may say, whether it is regarded by others as heretical, offensive, or even absurd, he/she has the right to say it, so long as he/she does not materially infringe upon the rights of others. To deny that right is to undermine seriously the whole concept of a democratic society." To my mind that anonymous justice should be enshrined as a minor hero in the pantheon of religious liberty.

The concept of radical soul liberty, as I have chosen to call it, involves a drastically different approach from that of religious toleration. It holds to the conviction that every human being, as a creation of God, is of infinite value and therefore divinely imbued with the right and the responsibility to work out his or her own relationship with God in an individual and unfettered way. No earthly authority, whether governmental or ecclesiastical, can override that natural, inborn right. Indeed, any effort to impose by external means religious belief on individuals is doomed to failure. Conformity of behavior can be coerced, but the

sanctuary of a person's soul is invulnerable. Human beings will finally choose what they believe, regardless of the pressures brought to bear upon them.

The concept of radical soul liberty has complex dimensions, and I can only briefly summarize some of them here. To hold to the right of one's own religious freedom is clearly to hold also to the equal right of every other person. Here the American Puritans failed to be consistent. Avidly jealous for their own freedom, they failed to extend that right to others, and at this point Roger Williams rightly departed from them, both theologically and geographically.

The problem of the Puritans was simple. They were irrevocably convinced that their interpretation of the Scriptures was absolutely correct, and they could brook no disagreement. Williams challenged them with a radically different interpretation, and they could not accept or tolerate it. Thus, religious freedom in New England was smothered under a majority religious imperialism, buttressed by legal and governmental authority.

No one has ever argued more persuasively for religious freedom than did the American Founding Father, James Madison, a primary moving force in the Bill of Rights. Setting himself against Patrick Henry's attempt to establish a kind of religious establishment in Virginia, he contended that to violate the separation of church and state would infringe upon the natural liberties of citizens; unbalance the equality among them; make civil magistrates judges of religious truth, which they are not competent to judge; corrupt the churches themselves; and jeopardize the multiculturalism that is fundamental to the American Dream. Those somewhat bizarre individuals who seek to argue today that the authors of the American Constitution did not specifically intend to prescribe church-state separation need to reread their Madison—or indeed read it for the first time.

Radical soul liberty, however, requires more from the religious believer than a simple adherence to the concept of church-state separation. It demands a positive affirmation of the religious freedom of every individual; regardless of his or her beliefs—or non-beliefs. I believe this affirmation carries with it the necessity—and this is a difficult area for many earnest Christians—to abandon the stance of religious imperialism: the unchallenged certainty that one is, religiously, totally and without any possibility of error in possession of truth.

We must live and act according to our certainties, but we must also live with our doubts. Our doubts remind us that, like the Apostle Paul, we see through a

glass darkly. We must live by the truth that we believe we know, but a realistic awareness of our human situation—that we are limited in our time-space box and likewise limited by our own pervasive sinful natures—means that we cannot claim rightly total knowledge of ultimate truth. That simply means that God, by definition, is bigger than any of us and that we cannot confine God in the narrow walls of our own confessions and catechisms. Radical soul liberty demands, therefore, the virtue of honest humility and a stance of openness to others who differ from us in spiritual understanding.

The abandonment of religious imperialism does not imply any form of wishy-washy religious compromise—a willingness to settle for the least common denominator in faith in order to achieve some sort of vaporous unity of all. That usually means a superficial mouthing of universal platitudes without substance. Every person is entitled to proclaim personal faith, as he or she understands it, thereby submitting it to the reasoned and experiential response of others. And, equally, every individual is entitled to "convert," to use a Christian term; that is, to alter, even drastically, his or her religious convictions, if he or she so chooses. An American should not be foreordained, by culture and tradition, to be a Christian; neither should a Muslim or a Hindu, a Buddhist or a Jew, be so ordained. Radical soul liberty will settle for nothing less than free, informed, personal religious choice.

Radical soul liberty includes the right of every individual to witness freely to his or her faith. This is where, for Christians, the Great Commission is important. We are commanded to tell others, wherever they may be, that our personal encounter with the Christ has brought us forgiveness, justification, joy, and peace—salvation. Wherever and whenever another human being responds to our witness and experiences those same things, that is the fulfillment of our mission. But we also have the obligation to listen to and learn from others, even those who most violently disagree with us. A person's individual choice is made more meaningful and lasting the more he or she understands the differing approaches to spiritual truth.

It may be salutary at this point for Baptists to remember that some of our denominational ancestors believed so strongly in the importance of mature, meaningful religious decision that they practiced only "adult baptism." Modern Baptists have largely retreated from that position, but I venture to suggest that many thinking Baptists today are sometimes concerned about the loose application of the

so-called "age of accountability." As for myself, I am willing to leave that decision to Christian pastors and congregations, but the principle remains intact.

The New Testament uses the Greek work *koinonia* to describe its fellowship of believers, living together in mutual respect and concern, bound by the underlying and supreme virtue of agapeic love—unselfish care for and concern for the other. *Koinonia* is a decisive term in the Christian community. Every person who has ever been a Christian pastor realizes that there is always a "church within the church"—an inner group of those who have more fully understood and accepted the demands of their faith. The *koinonia* is always and everywhere the prime source of whatever spiritual power is generated by the Christian church.

I believe the meaning of *koinonia* can be expanded without diminishing its special significance for the Christian community. There is, I think, a kind of potential *koinonia* of God-fearing, God-loving, God-seeking people in the world. The basic needs of people transcend their differences. Their vocabularies are vastly different, and their struggle for spiritual understanding takes many forms, but the "void in their souls," to use the words of St. Augustine, is identical. They want God and everything that implies. They seek God. "Seeker," incidentally, is a word that Roger Williams used to describe himself in his later days. Surely the loving God revealed in Jesus Christ cares for all these human souls and reaches out toward them.

I believe that, in their common humanity, God-lovers, God-fearers, and God-seekers have a possible ground on which to live together, love together, and learn together in the face of an increasingly secular world where all serious thought of God has been abandoned by so many.

Writing in 1952 in *The Irony of American History*, Reinhold Niebuhr made the point that "the most effective force for community is religious humility. This includes the charitable realization that the vanities of the other group or person, from which we suffer, are not different in kind, though perhaps in degree, from similar vanities in our own life. It also includes a religious sense of the mystery and greatness of the other life, which we violate if we seek to comprehend it too simply from our standpoint."

I venture to say that a recognition of this kind of *koinonia* could offer one of our best hopes in this tragically divided world. The challenge of secularism is rampant, and it offers no real solution to our problems—only more division, more hate, more

violence. Unhappily it is clear that many American Christians have forgotten what *koinonia* means. I think particularly of the bitter conflict among Baptists over secondary doctrinal issues. Mutual respect and Christian love have too often been thrown overboard in a raw struggle for power. Emotive ethical issues such as abortion have generated more heat and hatred than love and reasonable discussion. Insult, hostility, denigration, and violence are not the characteristics of a Christian community. The Body of Christ has been left and bleeding.

Not just in America, but around the world, the situation is much the same. Northern Ireland is supposedly a Christian community, but for many thousands of people in that unhappy province, any sense of *koinonia* between Protestants and Catholics has disappeared. Too often, the religious zealots on both sides are those who carry the banners of conflict. Beyond the bounds of nominally Christian areas—places like Bosnia, Serbia, and the Near East—any sense of human kinship and a shared responsibility as children of God is clearly absent, even among those who claim in one way or another to be children of God.

I wish I knew some magic formula to institute a movement to revive and renew a sense of koinonia, first of all, among my fellow Christians, but also among that larger community who seek God and good in the world. Sadly, I do not. I am convinced that there cannot be that badly needed spiritual awakening in our society without it. I can hope, and I can pray. I know that sounds idealistic. To dream of a world in which God-lovers, God-fearers, and God-seekers live and love and learn together is utopian, perhaps. But when in human history have we made any real progress without the persistent prodding of the idealists and the dreamers?

Let me close by emphasizing again my main points. Radical soul liberty is our basic human right. If we surrender that natural right, we will eventually surrender all other freedoms. The American Declaration of Independence proclaims that every human being is entitled to life, liberty, and the pursuit of happiness. Without radical soul liberty there can be no real life, no genuine liberty, no lasting happiness. But radical soul liberty is a universal right—one that cannot be sustained in our unhappy world without the development of a true sense of *koinonia*.

Religious freedom and *koinonia*—like love and marriage, horse and carriage—go together.

13

CONFESSIONS OF A LAPSED LUDDITE

(This article first appeared in Christian Ethics Today.*)*

The Luddites, as many will know, were a group of English craftsmen in the early nineteenth century who were alarmed because the introduction of technology into the English cloth industry meant that their jobs were under threat. They reacted violently, seeking to destroy the machines that undermined their ways of making a living. Their protest failed, of course, and the march of new technology went inexorably on.

I have never been a real Luddite. True, for many years I resisted the lure of the computer, despite the pitying glances of many of my friends. I was a bit of an outcast because I had no e-mail address. Finally, however, I succumbed and bought a computer. Now I have an e-mail address and use the computer for my writing (although this really gives me little more than my old word processor.) But I must admit that I like e-mail. It keeps me in touch with a lot of people with whom it is otherwise difficult to keep contact. I have never been seriously tempted to launch a violent, physical attack on machines, factories, or laboratories—all bastions of the new technology—though I have occasionally thought of taking an ax to my television set, especially when all I can get is Jerry Springer or Ricki Lake.

I do have, however, a nagging distrust of uncritical enthusiasm for any and all technological "advance." The convenient axiom in some scientific circles—"if it can be done, do it"—does not sit comfortably with me. I am old-fashioned enough to believe that, perhaps, there are some things we can do that, morally, we ought not to do. The problem is that computers and indeed all

technological devices are amoral. They are inanimate machines, however much they may mimic human behavior. They possess no ethical discrimination. Whatever morality is programmed into our technology is put there by human beings. And I am haunted by my biblical, and experiential, understanding that all human beings, whether they be computer programmers, scientists, technicians, or writers on ethical questions, are sinful beings. Whatever moral knowledge they feed into their machines arises out of their own moral sensibility, and that sensibility is always and everywhere suspect.

I want here to consider only one small part of the technological revolution, perhaps what some would consider a minor one. I have recently been concerned about the widespread use of video and computer games. A perceptive book has come to my attention. John Naisbitt, a presidential advisor to Kennedy and Johnson, is the author of *High Tech, High Touch*. His analysis of contemporary society is a sobering and thoughtful argument, and one of his most alarming sections describes the effect that interactive computer games are having on children.

The reach of these electronic games is staggering, with an audience affecting far more people than cinema or books. About 65 percent of American homes, according to Naisbitt, now possess such games, and nearly half of the players are under eighteen. Even more alarming is the fact that American children apparently possess an appetite for the most violent of these games, and this kind of game accounts for 70 percent of the market. Is it surprising that some of these games are being widely promoted with slogans such as "more fun than killing your neighbor's cat"?

I must acknowledge here my debt to Melanie Phillips, a columnist for the *London Times*, who has researched this area thoroughly. Children, quite obviously, are attracted to such games, and many of the games are advertised deliberately to target children. In 1998 an advertisement for a game called "Vigilance" encouraged children aged thirteen-plus to "put your violent nature to good use." The ad was illustrated by a picture of a boy's jean-clad legs, the barrel of a shotgun at his side, and two dead classmates at his feet. Some of the latest games feature rape, torture, and mass killings. By the time the players reach the highest level of the game "Carmageddon," they will have run over and "killed" 30,000 pedestrians.

Violence in popular culture is nothing new. We live in a gun-obsessed society. But these games are something else. They affect children in diverse ways. They provide them with the sensation of being active killers, and these sensations

are becoming increasingly realistic through the advances of technology. Soon the players will literally feel the "kick" of a fired gun, the impact of a blow, or the dripping of the victim's blood. They will hear the screams of pain and terror as they "kill" hundreds of people. Some games are being designed to toy with children's sanity, aiming to induce paranoia and deliberately confusing the child as to what is real and what is not.

The effect of such games is not only dramatic but addictive. Naisbitt quotes one source who believes that one out of four children who play become addicted. Very young children who can't tell reality from fantasy are easily hooked. Unlike ordinary television, such games engage children's entire attention as they are taken on an emotional roller coaster that rewards for killing or injuring people. Respected psychologists say that extended computer use is altering the physiology of children's brains, causing rising attention deficit disorders and depression. It is rearranging the ways their brains work and changing the emotional life of the child players.

Concrete evidence exists that virtual stimulation reality is usefully employed to treat phobic or traumatized patients by desensitizing them and reprogramming their reactions. Why are we reluctant to admit that this same technique can change individuals for the worse as well as for the better? The fact is that children over a period of time can be programmed to be callous killers.

Not surprisingly, the military establishment has been quick to take advantage of the technological opportunities. Soldiers are now being trained through electronic war games that provide high-tech simulation and conditioning. Laser engagement systems in which blank shots trigger laser pulses on soldiers' vests have spawned children's games such as "Laser Tag," whose sales in the United States reached 245 million dollars in 1998. Its derivative in ordinary action terms, "Paint Ball," provides interested individuals the opportunity to stalk and kill other individuals, without, of course, any actual physical damage. Is it surprising that this activity was reportedly used by the schoolboy killers at Columbine High School in Colorado to refine their skills for their later tragic attack? After another such incident in Paducah, Kentucky, it was revealed that the fourteen-year-old killer had fired with deadly accuracy because he had hours of practice on video games that had encouraged him to develop his skills to shoot people.

The close, though surely unintended, links between the military and the computer games industry, dubbed by Naisbitt the "military-Nintendo complex," are reflected in the fact that children are being induced to buy games for "the smell of napalm" or "the beautiful sound of your arsenal blowing away tanks." It is not surprising that modern war, projected to us on our television screens, has devised euphemisms for its most destructive actions. "Euphemisms" are, of course, polite words for unpleasant actions. Thus, we are told of "collateral damage," which means that innocent civilians have been killed, or "smart bombs," which are weapons presumably intended to reach their planned targets. What results is that play is becoming like war, and war is becoming like play. The harsh realities are neatly wrapped up in verbiage.

I am not one of those who posit a simple one-dimensional solution to our problems. After the recent terrible incidents of school violence in the United States, there were those who rushed forward with a single cause behind the actions. Some blamed everything on lax gun laws. Others picked out the movies or television as the culprit. Yet others singled in on what I have been discussing—violent computer games. The answer clearly does not lie in a single area. We face a larger cultural crisis. In an atmosphere dominated overwhelmingly by materialism and hedonism—one in which any overriding moral standard is foreign to so many people—these outbreaks of violence are not surprising.

If a culture has lost its moral way and has opted to discard or ignore the ethical and moral wisdom accumulated across the centuries, who can predict what terrible results will come? In a culture that exalts monetary gain above all other goals and pursues a consistent "feel-good" ethic in personal behavior, tragic and senseless events are inevitable. The decision to throw away all objective or universal standards of right and wrong can have only one final result—moral chaos.

I call attention here to only one aspect of what I see as contemporary moral stupidity. Obviously, our educational system has many problems. There are some "experts" who tell us that the answer is "a computer in every classroom." I do not oppose that idea. But the notion that putting information machines into the hands of our children will solve our problems is fatuous. True education is not simply a matter of being able, by the push of a button, to assemble all the facts. It was Walker Percy, the American novelist, who observed that if we persist in believing that education consists of the simple assemblage of facts, "we will rear a generation

of moral idiots." True education teaches people how to use facts and leads them on into the higher realm of ideas, concepts, and dreams. It can enable us and our children to unravel many of the mysteries of ordinary human experience, but it can and ought to confront us also with the stubborn areas of ultimate mystery, such as the meaning of life itself.

I inwardly cringe when I stand at the checkout counter of my local supermarket. Behind the counter is a young girl who can manipulate the keys of her machine, tabbing up my purchases accurately (I hope), but who gazes at me with heavily made-up, glazed eyes that give no indication of any interest in such things as truth, beauty, and love—or even in me, a human being and her customer. (Admittedly, I may be misjudging this particular individual. Somehow I do not think so.)

What seems to be missing for many people today is a sense of perspective. Human beings have created machines. Now the question is "Who is the ultimate master?" Machines are created to be used, not to dominate our existence. I know from experience that I can tap the right keys on my computer and call up an almost inexhaustible wealth of useful information. I also know that I can tap other keys and conjure up on my monitor screen the most depraved and utterly evil images of a sinful humanity. That is not the fault of my computer. I have pressed the keys, and other human beings have fed into the network the filth and dregs of their twisted and money-obsessed minds. It is the same old sorry story: powerful forces of evil at work through human beings in our world.

My wanderings in this article have led me considerably beyond my concern with the problem of violent computer games. My concern in that area remains the same, but the problem is far more extensive than that limited one. I have classed myself as a "lapsed Luddite." I am not a Luddite in the sense of sharing the illusion of the nineteenth-century workmen that they could solve their problem by destroying the mechanical weaving looms that threatened their livelihood. But I share with them a deeper and more instinctive fear, never verbally expressed or, perhaps, even realized by them. Despite all its benefits the machine can be ultimately an enemy of humanity. Whether it is or not is our responsibility.

I do firmly believe that there are some things technically possible that morally should not be done. Whether these things are done depends on the judgment of

human beings, and the validity of those judgments depends on the individual's moral sensitivity.

I would also remind us that machines are not infallible. Sometimes we become so obsessed with the machine that we give it a status it does not deserve. A somewhat ludicrous observation comes to mind. Part of the planned celebrations on Millennium Eve in London, England, where I presently live, was the inauguration of the "Millennium Wheel," a giant Ferris wheel, the largest in the world, located on the banks of the Thames River near the Houses of Parliament. It was due to begin turning at midnight on New Year's Eve in elaborate ceremonies attended by the Prime Minister. Despite all the publicity buildup, it didn't operate—all because of a "computer error" in the signal system. It took a month of readjustments before it eventually began to turn.

More seriously and tragically, not long after that a terrible train accident occurred near Paddington Station in central London. A number of people were killed and dozens injured. The exact cause has never been precisely determined, but the strong suspect is "computer error." Machines are always susceptible to mechanical error. We must recognize their limitations.

Thinking men and women, rightly concerned about the amoral age in which we have become involved, might take a lesson from popular culture. The most adequate image of the computer may not be the lovable robots who were the companions of Luke Skywalker in *Star Wars*, but the cool, inhuman voice of HAL, the computer run amok in Stanley Kubrick's epic film *2001*. One image lulls us into complacency; the other is a salient warning.

14

THE FEMALE OF THE SPECIES

(This article was first published in Christian Ethics Today.*)*

One Sunday morning several months ago I visited a small church located near where I live. The church met in a simple building and less than a hundred people were present for the service.

I felt comfortable and much at home. The hymns were familiar and the congregation sang enthusiastically. After the offering was collected, we stood and sang the Doxology. The minister preached a clear, concise sermon dealing with a basic facet of the Christian gospel, the meaning of the cross. At the conclusion of the sermon we sang a hymn of invitation. Two people responded to the call for commitment. A woman, already a Christian, came forward to place her membership in the church. A mature man made his profession of faith in Christ as his Savior.

I went away that morning satisfied. I had found what I needed and wanted—a genuine experience of worship and an encounter with the Spirit of God. But I also knew that there was something strikingly different about the service, something that after years of churchgoing, I was largely unaccustomed to. The preacher (and pastor) that morning was a gray-haired, sprightly woman. With fire in her bones and conviction in her voice she had preached the gospel—but, still, she was a female. For me, that was different.

I left that service musing, somewhat sadly, on the undeniable fact that many of our contemporary Christian denominations are violently divided on the issue of women in the pulpit. The Church of England, for instance, faces factional division because of its willingness to accept women pastors. My own

denomination, Southern Baptists, has officially adopted a statement of faith that bars such women as I heard that day from the pastorate. She, and her congregation, would be anathema.

The issue of women in the pulpit is not a new one. It has bedeviled the Christian community for centuries. I have been involved in discussions about this question with fellow pastors where there have been condescending remarks about the abilities of women in the pulpit. I have been reminded of the tongue-in-cheek comment of the eighteenth-century polymath, Samuel Johnson, who is reported to have said, "A woman's preaching is like a dog's walking on its hinder legs. It is not done well, but you are surprised to find it done at all." I dare say that Dr. Johnson, who was not a stupid man, might well have altered his opinion had he attended with me the service to which I alluded earlier in this article.

Inevitably, when I discuss this matter with my fundamentalist Christian friends, they will point to biblical passages that they believe support their point of view. I deeply respect that approach. Like them, I am a Bible-believing Christian. I accept the teachings of the Bible as an authoritative guide in matters of Christian faith and practice. But there is a basic difference between us.

While I understand and accept the Bible to be the written revelation of God's character and will, I do not give final or infallible authority to any human or organizational interpretation of the meaning of those Scriptures, whether that interpretation be the idea of any individual or the pronouncements adopted by a show of hands in an assembly or convention. Christians do not, or should not, worship a particular method of biblical interpretation; they worship the God who is revealed in the Bible—and the difference is important. The Scriptures are the written word, but the meaning of the words must always be understood and interpreted, and in this task there is a more important Word. The Apostle John declares in the beginning of his Gospel, "In the beginning was the Word, and the Word was with God, and the Word was God" (John 1:1). Obviously, John is not speaking here of the written word but of the Logos, the living Word, the Christ. That living Word is our final authority when it comes to matters of meaning and interpretation. Jesus said, "He who has seen me has seen the Father" (John 14:9). All of our scriptural exegesis must be undertaken in the shadow of the Logos, and we are not entitled to interpret particular passages of Scripture in ways that are inconsonant with the character and message of Christ. Every passage of Scripture must be

viewed through a singular prism. That prism is the Christ as revealed to us in the Scripture.

In the Southern Baptist gathering that adopted a resolution excluding women from the pulpit and the pastorate, one of its leaders is reported to have said, "If a woman claims she had been called to the pastorate, she is simply wrong. She has not been called. God does not contradict himself." While I disagree profoundly with the first part of that statement, I give my hearty "Amen" to the second part. God certainly does not contradict himself. It is precisely for that reason that I find the exclusion of women from pastoral ministry impossible to accept.

Many years ago, when I was a young student in a conservative Baptist seminary, I was taught certain basic principles of exegesis—the discipline of scriptural interpretation. Men like Ray Summers, Robert Daniel, Stewart Newman, and T. B. Maston—names that will ring a bell with some of my older Baptist readers—instructed me in ways of understanding Scripture that have served me well for over fifty years. I see no reason to desert those principles now.

One basic exegetical principle is that for a particular interpretation of a passage of Scripture, one must look at the whole of Scripture and its portrait of the character of God. In applying this principle we must take account of the fact that there is nothing in the Gospels, recounting the ministry of Jesus, that supports the idea that females are second-class citizens of the kingdom of God. Indeed, in his treatment of women, Jesus never discriminated in any way. It is quite clear that women were then, as they have always been, key figures in the Jesus movement. This is especially true in Luke's Gospel where the female followers of Jesus receive particular mention—Joanna, Susanna, and Mary Magdalene, women who traveled with Jesus and the male disciples, fully incorporated in the group.

Of course, Mary Magdalene is the most important of the female disciples, and in John's Gospel she is presented as a model of discipleship. She is, in a real sense, the apostle to the apostles, for she is the first to witness the resurrected Jesus at the tomb on Easter morning, and she is commissioned by the risen Lord to tell the other disciples that she has seen him (John 20). Long into the Middle Ages Mary Magdalene was revered as "apostolorum apostle," apostle to the apostles. Jesus accepted and treated males and females equally, and in this respect he clearly reflects the character of God.

The Apostle Paul reinforced this understanding of the character of God in one of his most forthright declarations, a passage of Scripture not often cited by those who wish to exclude females from the pulpit. In the Epistle to the Galatian church Paul emphatically avers that "There is neither Jew nor Greek, there is neither bond nor free, there is neither male nor female, for you are all one in Jesus Christ" (Gal 3:28). What the Apostle says here is absolutely consistent with the nature of God as revealed through Jesus Christ.

The God revealed to us through the living Word is one who makes no distinctions on the basis of gender. We often address God in our prayers as "Our Father," and I have no objection to that because it rightly emphasizes the caring concern of God. But that address in no way implies that God is a male sexual being. God transcends any sexual differentiation. In the same way that God is not black, white, yellow, red, American, Russian, Chinese, or African, God is neither male nor female. Medieval (male) artists pictured God as an old man with a long, white beard, but that is a totally inadequate presentation. By tradition, we use the male pronoun for God, but in the fundamental sense God wipes away all gender discrimination.

In the basic matter of salvation God certainly does not make such distinctions. Without regard to gender, or any other human difference, we are all equally invited to come to God. Indeed, it is this refusal on the part of God to make such distinctions, reinforced by the identical characteristics in the teaching of Jesus, that has enabled the Christian faith to make such a significant contribution to the ongoing struggle in the secular society about us against unfair discrimination on the basis of such factors as race and gender.

It is ironic that some Christians should uphold, within the church, a dictum that in effect makes females second-class citizens of the kingdom of God. The Christian affirmation that there can be no gender distinction has been a prime factor in the advance of our secular culture to the position that the majority of that culture holds today: males and females alike are entitled to equal treatment in every part of our society. I do not believe, though I cannot know for sure, that my Christian friends who disagree with me on this issue would support unfair discrimination against women in the marketplace. I do not think they would countenance unequal pay for equal work on the basis of gender or the exclusion of women from positions of leadership in business or government simply because they are female.

Yet, do they not realize that when the Christian church endorses this kind of gender discrimination within its own ranks, it unwittingly, perhaps, undergirds those in the secular society who would carry on such practices?

My teachers taught me a second basic principle of exegesis. This was the principle of consistency. If one is to interpret Scripture correctly, one must at the very least be consistent. If, for instance, one approaches Scripture with the conviction that every admonition of the Apostle Paul in the Epistles establishes a permanent and unchanging pattern for church practice, one is not entitled to pick and choose, selecting those parts of Scripture that are seen to be lasting definitions of Christian practice and those that are not. I cannot make this principle of exegesis fit the kind of interpretation that seems to be ordinary among my disagreeing Christian brethren. One of the most frequently cited Scriptural passages by my friends to support their position is 1 Corinthians 14:34. In that passage Paul says, "Let your women keep silent in the churches, for it is not permitted unto them to speak." Leaving aside the seemingly clear meaning of that passage to forbid women having any verbal part in church affairs, whether in the pulpit or not, that seems to settle the matter for my friends. But, if we are to be consistent, we must remember that in that same letter, Paul instructs his hearers just as clearly that "every woman that prays or prophesies with her head uncovered dishonors her head" (1 Cor 11:5). Doesn't this quite evidently mean that a woman who prays or prophesies (preaches) with her head covered is doing a perfectly honorable thing?

Can we ignore the fact that the Apostle in his first letter to Timothy instructs the people to whom he is writing that "women adorn themselves in modest apparel, with shamefulness and sobriety; not with braided hair, or gold, or costly array" (2:9)? In my long life in the church I have heard numerous sermons in which the preacher declared that women were not fit to be pastors or preachers, but I have never heard a sermon in which the preacher ordered his female listeners, on the basis of the Bible, to wear hats when they came to church, or to throw away the gold wedding rings their husbands had given them, or to discard the pearl necklaces given to them in love by their children, or not to commit the sin of coming to church with braided hair. Where is the consistency here? Why pick one admonition and ignore the rest?

At this point my friends argue that because God has assigned individuals differing roles in the church because of gender differences, Paul's instructions

concerning women must be understood in a different way from his other pronouncements. I can understand that argument up to a point. There are obvious physical and genetic differences between males and females, as God has created us. Males sire children; females bear children. That is undeniable. But, for the life of me, I have been unable to find any genetic or biological difference between males and females that supports the idea that men are, by virtue of their maleness, better preachers or pastors than women.

In my life I have known good male preachers and poor ones. I am sure that there are good female preachers and poor ones, but the difference is not genetic or sexual. Our individual callings from God to vocation are a matter of our individual talents and the degree of our surrender to the will of God. Some (both male and female) are called to preach; others are called to be missionaries; and others are called to be lay witnesses. The call of God extends to all human beings. It seems to me the height of spiritual arrogance for a male preacher to say that if a pious, dedicated woman understands God's call to her to be that of the ministry, he in his male role has the right to say that she is mistaken and wrong.

The third basic principle of exegesis that I learned was that one must always look at a particular passage of Scripture within its context. It is important to know when the passage was written and to whom it was written. Paul wrote his Epistles to particular Christian communities, operating within their own cultural context. Much of the body of the Epistles deals with fundamental issues in the understanding of Christian doctrine, but also much of Paul's writing is pastoral and practical advice on the special problems each of these communities faced. In approaching the exegesis of these passages we must always keep in mind Paul's primary purpose—the effective witness to the central truths of the gospel.

Perhaps the most instructive passage in this regard is Paul's advice to the Corinthian church regarding the eating of meats that had been offered to idols. Clearly, this was a problem peculiar to the Corinthians. Paul first makes it clear that there is no sin in eating such meat (1 Cor 8:8), then he gives his practical advice: "But take heed lest by any means this liberty of yours becomes a stumbling block to them that are weak" (8:9). His final counsel is "If meat make my brother to offend, I will eat no meat" (8:13).

If we apply our understanding of this passage to the interpretation of other such passages in the Epistles, certain things are clear. First, in dealing with

secondary matters of practice within the church, Paul's governing concern is what will further the cause of gospel witness. Second, in dealing with such matters Paul was willing, in his own day and time and in consideration of the pagan culture around him, to advise that the church adopt certain practices, not because there was any sin involved nor, I think, to lay down patterns for the future church, but to avoid offending unnecessarily that particular culture.

It is from this standpoint that I think we can better understand many of Paul's other admonitions to particular churches. Writing to another church in a somewhat different cultural situation, as I have previously mentioned, Paul advised the women in the church in Corinth not to appear in church with their heads uncovered, not to wear gold ornaments or jewelry, and not to braid their hair. Clearly, those practices, though morally neutral in themselves, would in Corinth have been hindrances to their witness. It must be remembered that in this same letter Paul advised women to keep silent in church.

When we seek to understand the cultural situation of the New Testament church, we must realize that the radical beliefs and practices of the church created a tremendous tension in its relationship with the pagan, predominantly Roman ethos in which it operated. The deeply egalitarian teachings of Jesus (the promise of salvation for all) totally contradicted the values of a hierarchical society, economically based on the labor of slaves. A vital part of that pagan society's structure was the subjugated and inferior position of women.

Christianity decisively challenged those pagan values. The Christian church not only allowed but also positively encouraged all human beings—slave and free, Jew and Gentile, educated and uneducated, men and women—to worship, live, and love together. It was especially this facet of the new faith that drew the scorn of Celsius, a prominent second-century pagan critic, who poured vitriolic scorn on Christians for such practices.

Jane Shaw, a widely respected church historian, in her McCandless lecture in March 2000 at Georgetown College in Kentucky, pointed out:

> Roman society had very distinct ideas about how a virtuous woman
> should behave; submissively, and certainly not speaking in public.
> Roman law held that by nature women were the weaker sex, they

lacked seriousness, and they therefore required the authority of men (husbands and fathers) over them.

It is surely with an awareness of these pagan surroundings that a sensible exegesis of Paul's strictures against women must be seen. Remembering always the Apostle's primary concern with effective Gospel witness, it is not surprising that, as with eating meat to idols, he would advise particular church congregations not to offend unnecessarily the overwhelmingly male-dominated society in which they operated.

The biblical, historical, and archeological evidence suggests that women held the principal leadership offices, alongside men, for the first three centuries, at least, of Christianity. In many early Christian communities women, as well as men, were deacons, presbyters (priests), bishops (episkopei—overseers), apostles (missionaries), teachers and prophets. Throughout the New Testament, we get tantalizing glimpses of this reality. When Paul wrote to the Christians in Rome, it is deacon Phoebe who carries his letter to them and thereby introduces Paul to them. She was his patron. He concluded his letter to the Romans by greeting the leaders in the Christian community there, among whom there were many women. Ten out of the twenty-eight whom he greets are women: Prisca, Mary, Tryphena, Persis, Julia, Olympas, the mother of Rufus, the sister of Nercus, and Junia. Especially prominent among these women was Junia, "prominent among the apostles," with her husband, Andronicus, whom Paul had known when he was in prison.

Dr. Shaw continues:

Paul says . . . in his first letter to Timothy, in which he describes a bishop or overseer as being like a householder—he must manage his household well . . . for if someone does not know how to manage his household, how can he take care of God's church? In this letter Paul assumes that the householder is male, but his own travels and missionary activities had shown him otherwise. For example, when he arrived

in Philippi, as recounted in Acts 16, he preached to a woman named Lydia, a dealer in purple cloth, a woman of reasonably substantial means and a householder. When she converted to Christianity, so the rest of her household was baptized too (Acts 16:15). And when Paul was released from prison, as recounted at the end of chapter 16 (verse 40), it was to Lydia's house that he went, so that he could meet and worship with other Christians before he left the city.

Actually, this pattern of essential female involvement in the church has continued through the centuries, despite great pressure from the male-dominated society in which it has existed. I know from my own experience as a pastor that no modern church could function without the dedicated efforts of Christian women. We have traditionally entrusted them to teach our children in Sunday school the fundamentals of the Christian faith. They have volunteered by thousands to be missionaries on the home and foreign fields. True, Paul advised the Corinthian church not only that women should keep silent in churches, but that, if women want to learn anything, they should "ask their husbands at home" (1 Cor 14:35). Incidentally, in fifty years I have never heard a sermon on that text. In actual fact several of the finest Bible teachers and expositors I have heard have been women, including a marvelous woman who taught for many years a mixed Bible class of men and women in the church I pastored. My sister, Faye Robbins, is a gifted teacher of the Scripture, and her ministry in various churches has through the years been blessed and productive. The arbitrary exclusion of females from the offices of preacher and pastor does not, for all these reasons and many more, make sense to me.

I think the final and perhaps most decisive point to be made in this argument is to go back to the Apostle Paul himself. As I have repeatedly pointed out, Paul was governed in all his actions by one decisive consideration: the effective witness to the gospel. Paul lived and wrote in a male-dominated society. He was willing, for the sake of the gospel, to make certain concessions to that culture.

We live today in totally different cultural surroundings. The secular culture, with which we have to deal as Christians, is one that is, at least in its majority opinion, committed to sexual and gender equality. We should rejoice in that. Christians have helped to bring that about. Now, if we apply Paul's guiding

principle, we must decide what will most effectively serve the cause of Christian witness. To maintain the stance of gender discrimination within the church, it seems to me, seriously harms our witness. On this basis I dare say that the counsel of Paul to the Corinthian church would be very different from the counsel he would give to the church in Nashville or Atlanta or Dallas.

I cannot close without another reference to the worship experience I described in the opening paragraphs of this article. When the gospel is preached and when the Holy Spirit evidently blesses that proclamation with the salvation of a soul, who will label that experience "un-Christian" simply because the preacher was a woman?

Protestants do not, unlike their Catholic brethren, pick out particular individuals in their history and designate them as "saints." But if, in particular, Baptists did have saints, I think the list would include Lottie Moon and Annie Armstrong, two intrepid Christian missionaries for whom annual missions offerings are named. I should imagine that if by some miracle Annie Armstrong and Lottie Moon were to return to us in the flesh, it would be a brave and, I think, foolish pastor who would deny them his pulpit to tell their stories and give their witness, even though they are quite clearly "females of the species."

15

TRUTH-TELLING: AN EXERCISE IN PRACTICAL MORALITY

(This article originally appeared in Christian Ethics Today.*)*

Any respectable list of aphorisms must include the time-honored words "Honesty is the best policy." Most of us pay sincere lip service to that admonition, but in everyday life the translation of those words into action can often present a puzzling challenge.

I was reared in a Christian home. My parents instructed me always to tell the truth, and I was sometimes punished when I failed to do so. I identified truth with the facts of the matter, insofar as I knew them. The apocryphal tale of George Washington was a familiar story. "I cannot tell a lie. I chopped down the cherry tree," the future "Father of our Country" declared, to the moral applause of ensuing generations.

I began my formal schooling with a firm conviction that it was always right to tell the truth, but I soon faced a worrying problem. Clearly, to many of my fellows there was something dishonorable and unmanly about being a "tattletale"—telling the truth about some blameworthy act committed by another person. Thus arose one of my first small moral dilemmas. Was it more virtuous always to tell the truth or should one tactfully hold one's tongue in certain situations? That this was not just a childish problem was brought home to me in my later years as a college professor when I witnessed students struggle seriously with the decision as to whether to report another student for cheating on an examination.

American high schools in my day usually presented a "junior" and a "senior" play each year (some may still do so).

I played a small part in my senior play. The play was a popular potboiler titled "Nothing But the Truth." The slender plot revolved around a decision by a group of people to speak nothing but the truth—the facts—for a specified period of time. As the drama progressed, scenes of comedy, chaos, and even tragedy were depicted, all as the result of rigid truth-telling.

My role in that play did not make me a theatrical star, but it did start some wheels turning in my mind. Is honesty really always the best policy? Is it universally wrong to tell a lie, regardless of the consequences? Are there such things as "white lies" that are morally acceptable in contrast to other lies that are not?

Some years after my high school days I became a soldier in the United States Army during World War II. As part of my military training I was told that, if I should be captured, I was obliged under the Geneva Convention to tell the enemy only my name, rank, and serial number. I was also instructed that in certain circumstances it would be appropriate to supply the enemy with false information. As a simple illustration, if I were asked about the rate of casualties in my unit, it would be acceptable for me to say that the rate was very low, even if, in fact, more than half of my unit had been killed or wounded in recent fighting. This, I was told, was a "useful lie." Are useful lies morally acceptable?

I have dredged up these random reflections from my own experience in order to make the point that truth-telling, as a practical moral exercise, is often far from simple. Christians regard the Old Testament Decalogue as a God-given and dependable basis for moral conduct. The ninth commandment tells us that we are not to bear false witness against our neighbor. At this point we are faced with the inevitable problem of interpretation. The commandment is stated in human language. What do the words mean when applied to real-life situations? A narrow understanding of the meaning of "bearing false witness" might be that it forbids us to falsify facts when giving testimony under oath in a court of law. But both Jews and Christians have understood the commandment to extend much further, placing upon us a general moral obligation to tell the truth.

Does this understanding of the commandment relieve us of difficulty by dictating a simple, uncomplicated duty to tell the factual truth under any and all circumstances? It would be comfortable to think so, but my life experience leaves me with nagging problems. One of those problems is the definition of truth. That, of course, is an age-old question. Even Pontius Pilate asked, "What is truth?"

Is there more to truth than simply the replication of facts? Is the ninth commandment our final moral authority in this area? What are we to do if it seems that the obligation to tell the factual truth conflicts with another commandment, such as that of Jesus that we should love our neighbor as ourselves?

In the eighteenth century, the philosopher Immanuel Kant dealt with the overall moral problem involved in telling the truth. Relying on philosophical reasoning, he insisted that indeed truth is identical with facts and, further, that woven into the fabric of the universe are certain moral absolutes that he called "categorical imperatives." One of those imperatives is the necessity to tell the truth under any imaginable circumstance. His only concession was to say that it may sometimes be acceptable to remain silent.

Ever since Kant, ethicists have debated his conclusions. They have worried, for instance, over a sample application of Kant's position. In modern terms the situation is this. Suppose that you are in the front yard of your house, trimming your hedge. Out of the house next door runs your neighbor's wife, obviously terrified. She dashes into your yard and hides herself behind the hedge. Seconds later, she is followed by her irate husband, brandishing a hatchet. He calls out to you, "Did you see my wife? Where did she go?"

The facts are clear. You do know where she is. Are you obliged to tell her husband the truth? Kant would grant only that you have the option to remain silent. Is that the best thing to do in this situation? Would it possibly be better to point down the street and say, "She went that way"? To say those words would be to lie in terms of the actual facts, but it might well buy you time to get the wife into the safety of your house and even to call the police. Of course, some "macho" types might suggest that you tackle the angry husband and take the hatchet away from him, but not all of us are supermen. I do not choose at this point to try to solve that moral dilemma. I use the story simply to raise questions.

Some thirty years ago an American theologian, Joseph Fletcher, published a book that for a brief period caused a stir in religious circles. The book was called *Situation Ethics*, and it set forth the argument that what we call moral absolutes are not absolutes at all but only general moral guidelines. Fletcher believed that every actual situation of moral choice is almost completely unique. It is the context of action—the "situation"—that dictates the right action. What is good in one situation may be bad in another. Fletcher went on to argue that, for the Christian, there

is finally only one moral absolute—agape love, the love Jesus taught and exemplified.

Fletcher's presentation left large logical gaps, and his critics were quick to point these out. The overwhelming number of human moral decisions are not nearly so unique as Fletcher believed. The similarities among decision-making situations are, by and large, more important than the supposed uniqueness. Fletcher was accused of, in actuality, discarding almost completely the moral wisdom of such dicta as the Ten Commandments. In addition, he seemed to fail to take seriously the ingrained propensity of men and women to interpret his sole absolute—love—in twisted and perverse ways. It is not enough to instruct individuals "to do the loving thing"; that command leaves people with a possibly suspect and highly subjective standard. Fletcher's arguments faded into obscurity, leaving only the term "situation ethics" as a convenient whipping post, especially for many conservative moralists.

Several years before Fletcher, another theologian, Dietrich Bonhoeffer, raised more searching questions, especially in the area of truth-telling. Bonhoeffer took as his central concern the question "What is truth?" Is truth simply a replication of the facts or is it something more than that? He sought to put the understanding of truth within a larger context—the loving purposes of God in the world as exemplified in Jesus Christ. Well aware of human sinful tendencies, Bonhoeffer did not discard the moral injunction that it is always right to tell the truth, but he refused to identify truth with bare facts. Truth is always and everywhere, Bonhoeffer thought, consistent with the compassionate purposes of God. To be "true," therefore, a word or act must be somehow loving and redemptive.

Like Fletcher, Bonhoeffer argued (on far more solid ground, I think) that the situation or context of an action is important in determining the right or wrong thing to do or say. No moral decision can be divorced from the circumstances in which it is made. The concrete situation assists us in applying the love-ethic of Jesus and in determining what is actually redemptive in real-life situations. Like Fletcher, Bonhoeffer insisted that the supreme moral commandment is to love our neighbor as ourselves. Unlike Fletcher, he did not want to cast away the moral wisdom of the Ten Commandments. Their guidance is of indispensable value in helping to understand what is actually redemptive and compassionate. In the area

of truth-telling, for instance, the burden of proof is heavily on any person who decides to depart from the facts of the matter.

How then do we arrive at the truth, in Bonhoeffer's sense of that word, in a specific decision-making situation? Bonhoeffer argued that one significant component of truth is that it must be "coherent" with the actualities of the situation. To put this simply, if one is called on to answer a question, it is important to try to understand what is the questioner is actually asking. Perhaps this idea can be clarified with three examples, one rather minor and oft-used, the other two more serious.

Suppose that you are a husband greeting your wife who has just returned from a shopping expedition. She goes into the bedroom and shortly returns, having put on an expensive new dress that is the fruit of her shopping. She models it before you and then asks, "Do you like it?" In this particular situation, imagine that you actually do not like the dress. If fact, you do not like it at all. What do you say to your wife? Do you tell the truth—that is, give her the facts?

Bonhoeffer suggests that it is important in this situation to understand what the wife's question means. She obviously likes the dress; otherwise she would not have bought it. Is she asking for your honest opinion? Or is she asking for your support for an action that she has already carried out? Would any loving or redemptive purpose be served by your giving her the full blast of your negative views?

Granted, the "right" answer will depend a great deal on the personalities of the two people involved. If the relationship is such that the husband knows his actual opinion is important to his wife and that she will have no difficulty accepting his opinion, then it might be best to give her the facts. My judgment is that there are many marital relationships where more harm than good would be done by giving a brutal, honest opinion.

In a more serious situation, consider a doctor attending a patient who is terminally ill, according to all of the available medical knowledge. The patient asks the doctor, "Am I going to die?" What does the doctor say? Does he or she simply impart the tragic facts, or is there a morally acceptable alternative?

I have discussed this situation with several of my Christian doctor friends. I am impressed that in every case my friends have said, in one way or another, "It would depend upon the situation." They seem to be saying that an important factor in their decision would be "What is the patient really asking?" Some people

would be asking for the bare facts of the matter, and they should certainly be given those facts. But others are not asking for that. They require some kind of support, some sort of hope, else their last days may well be horrible and unbearable. Should not the sensitive, caring physician frame his or her answer in a way that, even though it is not entirely consistent with the facts, contributes redemptively and lovingly to the welfare of the patient?

I would offer one other example that comes out of my experience years ago as a pastor and counselor. A sincere Christian young man, recently married, came to his pastor for advice. He told me that as a teenager, long before his marriage, he had led a dissolute and promiscuous sexual life. He had become a Christian, repented his sexual sins, and felt that God had forgiven him and wiped his moral slate clean. Now his conscience was troubled. Did he have a moral obligation to tell his wife the whole story about his past?

How would you have counseled this young man? Of course, again, a judgment must be made, imperfect at best, as to the character of the people involved. Acting on my best judgment, my advice to the young husband was that there was nothing to be gained, in terms of the supreme importance of his relationship with his wife, by giving her all the facts. It seemed to me that such a response might have done irrevocable damage to that relationship. I did not think that his wife either wanted or needed to know the "truth."

I realize how open to criticism I am at this point. There is the possibility, remote but real, that at a later date the wife may have learned that her husband had never given her all the facts. But I gambled on the belief that, even if that happened, the husband could justify his action on the basis of his love for his wife and his overwhelming desire to maintain the marriage relationship at its best. What seemed to me most important in the situation was not the facts but the people involved. Looking back, I feel more comfortable with my decision now, since that particular marriage has happily endured for almost forty years.

I have used these illustrations to point to the fact that decisions about "truth-telling" are not always simple and straightforward. Where does this leave us as Christians? Are we totally at sea when it comes to deciding whether or not to tell the "truth"? I think not. First, it is clear that we are not free to play fast and loose with the facts. The ninth commandment is not only a basic moral guideline, it is also an essential component of society. We could not operate unless we were

reasonably certain that, in all ordinary cases, people told us the factual truth. Chaos would result if, when we asked someone on the street what time it was, we had always to wonder whether they deliberately gave us the wrong answer.

The law is essential in the operation of ordinary life. But this does not allow for the extraordinary circumstances that sometimes present themselves. Thus, there is a second basic proposition. The law, however practical in ordinary circumstances, does not cover everything. Legalistic adherence to the letter of the law is not sufficient. Here, Christians must turn as always to the teaching of Jesus.

Clearly Jesus put love above law. He said that he had come to "fulfill" the law. To me that means that he came to give the law new meaning—a meaning that derives from the priority application of "Jesus-love" to the dimensions of the law. Jesus did not hesitate to violate the letter of the law if it conflicted with the demands of love and compassion. He ignored the Sabbath restrictions in order to heal the sick and suffering. Even more significantly, in the case of the woman taken in adultery, he put compassion first. The law prescribed the death penalty, but Jesus defied that woman's self-righteous accusers and said to her, "Go and sin no more." He acted redemptively and, thus, "fulfilled" the law.

Strict legalism always involves its practitioners in a maze of conflicting demands and illogical conclusions. In a particular situation two or more laws may seem to contradict each other. To be certain of rigid obedience to a law, its meaning and implications must be spelled out in great detail, as with the Jewish regulations for Sabbath observance. In practice, if not always in theory, this narrow stance lacks understanding that in the final analysis living people are more important than dead laws.

What I am suggesting here does not provide a simple method of making moral decisions, either in the specific area of "truth-telling" or in other situations of choice. Difficult judgments must be made. One must not narrow the range of love or unrealistically individualize it. In the case of a crime, for instance, God's love must be acted out, not only toward the criminal, but also toward the victim and, indeed, toward society as a whole. The demands of justice must be factored into the moral equation.

Doing the loving thing is, therefore, rarely easy and often risky. One could argue that with the woman taken in adultery, Jesus took a sort of moral gamble, trusting in the redemptive power of love and forgiveness to make the woman a

better person. There was no absolute assurance of that actually happening, but Jesus obviously felt the risk was worth taking. Crucial moral decisions by Christians almost always carry an element of risk, but I believe we are called to be daring in the name of love.

To return, finally, to our earlier Kantian illustration, I have decided upon reflection that when the angry husband rushed out of his house, I would have said to him, "She went that way," pointing in the wrong direction. Factually, that would have been a lie. But I hope I am not self-righteous when I say that, at that moment, I believe Jesus might have smiled.

16

"If It Feels Good, Do It"

(This article first appeared in Christian Ethics Today.*)*

Years ago, in an introductory university class in Christian ethics, I asked my students during the first days of the class to write a personal response paper answering from their own viewpoints two of the most pertinent questions in any ethical discussion: (1) how does one decide the difference between good and bad, and (2) what is the "good" life?

As one would expect, since a number of the students came from a north Florida conservative Christian background, some gave orthodox answers. Some determined what was good or bad by reference to the Ten Commandments or, in several cases, by asking the question "What would Jesus do?" Other students presented the fairly common response: what helps people is good, what hurts people is bad.

There were, of course, other answers. Some were superficial, but the paper submitted by one young man attracted my attention. Three things were evident from the paper: he was not an orthodox Christian, he had given some serious thought to the question, and he had been exposed at some point to a bit of philosophical thinking. He argued that the difference between good and bad comes down to a question of pleasure. The good is pleasant; the bad is painful. Therefore, the good life is one that produces pleasure and personal satisfaction and avoids pain. He ended with the following comment: "I want to live a life I can enjoy. That would be a good life."

That incident occurred long before the modern pop slogan "If it feels good, do it" became a catchphrase. My student's ideas were a prelude to what is today a widespread phenomenon:

the elevation of personal pleasure to the position of primary arbiter in moral deci-sions about human conduct.

Arguing against that moral stance presents some difficulties, at least to many moderns. Is there a sustainable reason why men and women should not do what is pleasurable? Does it make sense for human beings deliberately to submit them-selves to pain, or at least to the deprivation of pleasure?

My former student was a harbinger of things to come, but he was not an orig-inal thinker. In the fourth century BC, the Cyrenaics, a minor school of Greek philosophy headed by Aristippus, taught that all moral knowledge is unreliable and useless. The only thing we can clearly experience is the obvious difference between pleasure and pain. Therefore, the pursuit of immediate pleasure is the chief pur-pose of life, and sensual enjoyments are preferable, both to the more complicated and subtle joys of intellectual life and the rigors of moral restraint. Indeed, one of the disciples of Aristippus, Hegesias, taught that since pleasures are rare at best, the avoidance of pain should be the main concern of the wise and that suicide is by far the most efficacious way to avoid pain—the ultimate philosophy of despair.

I mention the Cyrenaics not as a kind of academic showoff, but simply to emphasize that there really is "nothing new under the sun." A contemporary of Aristippus, and a far more respectable philosopher named Epicurus, embraced the same idea of pleasure as the principal aim of life but sought to refine that idea by arguing that some pleasures are better than others—that intellectual pleasures, for instance, are more desirable than purely physical ones. From him we get the term "epicure," which the dictionary defines as "a person of refined and fastidious taste." Thus, for Epicurus a "good man" was someone who lived for pleasure but was smart enough to know which pleasures were best.

This kind of "feel-good" philosophy did not, however, vanish with the Greeks. In the nineteenth century, the influential English thinker Jeremy Bentham worked out a complicated system that, while still embracing pleasure as the main aim of life, sought to classify all pleasures. Bentham, a mathematician, devised a complex and, finally, impractical scale by which he thought all pleasures could be meas-ured—evaluating pleasure on the scale of intensity, purity, certainty, and fruitfulness. John Stuart Mill, Bentham's most influential disciple, refined this phi-losophy into a social one, positing that the "greatest good for the greatest number" was the ultimate aim of all good social policy. Good, of course, basically means in

this context pleasure, and pleasure is then defined as that which is most useful; that is, that which produces the most pleasure for the most people. This philosophy came to be called Utilitarianism. That style of thinking is still very much with us today.

The problem is that the great majority of people do not pause before making their moral decisions to think about philosophy. Here arises a prime defect in the approach of high-minded thinkers such as Bentham and Mill. The thoughtful person of integrity may take time in a cloistered study to weigh out carefully the consequences of his or her actions, seeking to find "the greatest good for the greatest number," but the ordinary person in the street tends by and large to look only at the immediate payoff in terms of pleasure.

What this means is that in actual practice the utilitarian philosophy comes down to each individual's interpretation. Since "greatest good" is translated as "greatest pleasure," decisions about conduct are often made on immediate and shallow grounds. Here is where a hard-nosed understanding of the Christian faith comes into play. The biblical Christian must insist on a fundamental and experiential understanding of human nature. To put it simply and scripturally, "all have sinned and come short of the glory of God." This is not an optimistic or happy view of humanity, but it is a realistic one. When the average human being, "the man on the Clapham omnibus," as British thinkers refer to him—John Doe— makes his moral decisions, those decisions are not surprisingly usually solipsistic and short of social responsibility.

In modern times sex has been elevated to the position of the most important of human activities. The media apparently believe that neither toothpaste nor coffee can be effectively advertised without a veneer of sexuality and the injection of sexual innuendo. As a result the most obvious area for consideration in this type of analysis is that of decisions regarding sexual conduct. The steadily growing number of illegitimate children, the increasing incidents of abortion, the multitude of people who live together without benefit of any religious or legal ceremony of marriage—all these statistics supply ample evidence. For a huge number of people in our contemporary society, sexual pleasure takes precedence over almost everything else. The social consequences—the greatest good for the greatest number—play little part in their decisions. Pleasure is the prime factor.

I happen to believe strongly in the right of a woman to control her own body and its reproductive functions, but I also believe that with this right come consequent responsibilities. If abortion is routinely seen as the "easy" way out—though, in actuality, it is far from easy—we open a Pandora's box. Abortion, from an objective viewpoint, should never be accepted as an escape hatch from sexual irresponsibility, yet that is what it seems to be for many today. Likewise, purely individualistic sexual behavior of any sort, entered into with no feeling of social consequences, is a serious danger for society as a whole.

We must not deceive ourselves, however, into thinking that sex is the only moral problem in our modern society. We live in an entrepreneurial age, and the self-made man, economically speaking, is our hero. To be rich—to "make it" economically—has been established as the final hallmark of success. Our consumer-oriented society encourages us to value economic achievement—sometimes, no matter how achieved—as the most admirable of all goals. This means that material prosperity has been equated with the highest pleasure, and the "if it feels good, do it" philosophy reigns supreme.

In a time in which all of us are bombarded with television advertisements and so-called entertainment programs that constantly tell us happiness consists in what we can buy, is it surprising that the underclass in our society who cannot financially afford all the luxuries they see paraded before them on television decide to steal or loot them? If pleasure is the end of all life, and if pleasure means the acquisition of material goods, then why not use any means to obtain them? Why should others have them when you do not? The "greasy thumbprint" of human sin leaves its mark here as everywhere.

Strangely enough this kind of "feel-good" approach to matters of sexual and economic ethics does not lack its academic defenders. In a lecture last year at the University of Toronto, the respected cultural commentator Michael Ignatieff argued that radical selfishness is an expression of moral virtue. Human beings, he said, have a prime duty to themselves and a prime right to individual freedom and happiness (pleasure). Ignatieff did not hesitate to face the consequences of his belief. We must, he said, accord respect to an individual's needs "against the devouring claims of family life." It is difficult if not impossible to see how Ignatieff's ideas jibe with the demands of such thinkers as Bentham and Mill for the "greatest good for the greatest number."

Ignatieff's approach seems, frankly, to be terribly naive. When a fifty-year-old male, struggling with his second adolescence, leaves his wife and children in cavalier fashion for the charms of a sexy, younger secretary, he has not exemplified legitimate human freedom. He has acted out of base irresponsibility, however it might be embellished with high-sounding appeals to the ideal of human freedom. What he has done is not something that affects only him but something that directly affects his wife—another human being deserving of respect—and his innocent children. Beyond that, he has affected in a real way the society in which he lives, the community of which he is an inseparable part. In reality he cannot separate himself and the effects of his action from the world about him. (I do not need to say, I trust, that these same words would apply to a woman who did something similar.)

The critical fact about the "feel-good" philosophy is that it ignores any sense of an over-arching moral imperative that places limits upon the exercise of personal freedom in the name of community responsibility. Individual freedom is a precious moral right, but freedom without responsibility has no moral basis. To act with no understanding that one's actions inevitably impinge at some point upon the freedom of others is the road to moral anarchy. With moral anarchy there is no community, and with no community there is no civilization.

Perhaps no thinker has viewed the human situation with more pessimism than the seventeenth century English philosopher Thomas Hobbes. Hobbes, not himself an orthodox Christian, embraced a view of human nature that carried ultra-Calvinism and its doctrines of original sin and total depravity to their ultimate. Human life in its natural state, said Hobbes, is a jungle existence. All individuals are depraved, brutish, totally self-centered, and interested finally only in their own survival and pleasure. Left in that state, all humans would be involved in a continuous war against each other—each seeking his own, victory to the strongest and annihilation to the weak.

Given that human situation, what is the answer? Hobbes had no faith in the power of moral ideals or of the grace of God to alter human beings in their conduct and moral choices. Thus, he followed his thinking to its logical conclusion. The only hope for humanity is what he called a "social contract," an agreement into which, for the sake of order and survival in the midst of chaos, human beings enter, entrusting their survival to the absolute rule of a political state, a

"Leviathan" that will ruthlessly enforce order on all its citizens, paying no attention to such values as individual freedom. The shape of that order will depend totally on the will of the rulers in power, and since those rulers are themselves, like their subjects, corrupted human beings, that order may well be tyranny of the worst order. Hobbes hoped for beneficent rulers, but the history of the twentieth century has taught us that, in the name of order, dictatorial rulers like Hitler and Stalin may seek to impose the most diabolical kind of structure upon their people, all in the name of the "greatest good for the greatest number."

To move from the "feel-good" idea to the extremes of Nazism and Communism may seem like a giant step, but the logic is inexorable. Unless there is some limit on the idea of totally individualistic pleasure as a moral principle, the door is open to almost unimaginable consequences—which we have seen worked out in terrible detail in our own lifetimes.

Even in a democratic society like our own, still guided to some extent by a sense of moral imperative, the dangers are fully apparent. True, and I think understandably, those less powerful elements in our society, whether they be economic, ethnic, or social, feel that they have no alternative except to organize themselves into power blocs of their own, more nearly equipped to oppose discrimination and oppression. Yet, if these new power groups are concerned only with their own selfish welfare—their own "pleasure"—with no regard for the rights and aspirations of those outside their blocs, the result can only be a continuance of injustice. The political, social, economic, and racial structure of society may be turned upside down eventually, but one oppressive group will only have been substituted for another.

The "feel-good" ethic is inevitably self-defeating. The individual or group that lives only its own pleasure will eventually face the situation in which its pleasure is opposed by another individual or another group with more power, and the individual's or group's pleasure will be replaced by misery. When power becomes the only ingredient in the social process, the weak must inevitably suffer.

I want to close this article with an idea that deserves much more attention than I can give it here. I do not for a moment accept the idea that pleasure is the final measure of moral action, but I do believe that there is a way to apply even this deficient principle to the Christian life. The word "joy" occurs in the Scripture innumerable times. When Jesus said in the Sermon on the Mount that the

peacemakers, the meek, the merciful, those who hunger after righteousness "are blessed," I do not think he meant that their reward would come only in the after-life. "Blessed" can be translated as "joyful," and I believe that there is joy—yes, pleasure—for the sincere Christian believer in this life, as well as in the life beyond. I have often heard the Christian life preached as if it were inevitably full only of suffering, pain, and self-denial. I reject that picture. True, there often comes pain, and certainly self-denial, if one seeks to live the Christian life. But there is infinitely more. I know from personal experience that there is real joy—certainly a kind of pleasure—in believing that one is striving to do the will of God. I know too many happy Christians to deny that. I know that there is a joy that comes from expanding one's moral horizons beyond animalistic self-interest to a concern for the neighbor. To love God, and to love one's neighbor, is not a trial but can be a blessing. The joy—the pleasure—that comes from a new focus of life and activity is something that cannot be measured in Bentham's calculus. I cannot help but pity my friends and fellow human beings who have never experienced that joy.

17

BIG GOVERNMENT:
A FRANKENSTEIN MONSTER?

(This article originally appeared in Christian Ethics Today.)

The specter of "big" government is constantly conjured up today by influential elements of the American polity. Government is depicted as a Frankenstein monster, completely out of control. Big government has become a red-flag phrase, painting a fearsome picture of an almost diabolical American government involved in a gigantic conspiracy designed to eliminate the basic rights and freedoms of all Americans. For some, the valid issues that should be part of rational discussion about any proposed piece of legislative action are immaterial. The action can be opposed on the simplistic grounds that it is another manifestation of big government.

A few extreme political paranoids have barricaded themselves in mountain fortresses, awaiting with fanatic certitude that day when the United States government will make its move, acting, some of them say, as the agent of Satan in the final Armageddon.

Most Americans, of course, do not go to that extreme. Still, many of us, bombarded daily by rabble-rousing radio talk shows (which show scant regard for the truth), some sections of the media, and the inflammatory rhetoric of some politicians, are susceptible to the supposed nightmare of big government. Without ever having actually read George Orwell's prophetic tract *1984*, many seize on his terminology and talk of "Big Brother," a secret government listening in on our every thought and steadily moving toward control of our every action. Had they actually read Orwell's book, they would realize the vast gap

between his vision of the possible future and what is actually happening in democratic America.

Frankly, I sometimes feel as if I am wandering in Alice's wonderland. Recently, at an ordinary suburban dinner party, I listened with amazement as a seemingly sane, well-educated, successful businessman told his dinner companions that when the United Nations was founded in 1946, it was part of an international conspiracy by certain powerful unnamed plotters to establish a totalitarian world government. I bit my tongue, partly out of polite respect to my hosts, but also because I long ago concluded that facts and reason mean nothing to someone with a fanatical, irrational obsession.

Does a concerned Christian citizen have anything relevant to say about the problem of big government? I think so, and I believe also that to speak out on matters like this one is a part of our Christian moral responsibility.

Christians live in two worlds. Jesus recognized this when he counseled, "Render unto Caesar those things which are Caesar's, and unto God those things which are God's." Some people understand that to mean there is a firm wall between sacred and secular responsibility. Not so. As citizens of the kingdom of Heaven, we are constrained to abide by the moral teachings of Jesus, but those same moral injunctions also apply to the secular area where they must be applied in effective ways.

The nineteenth century evangelist Dwight L. Moody once preached a sermon in Chicago in the course of which he launched a vigorous attack on corruption in municipal government. Afterward an angry woman from the congregation approached Moody, asking accusingly, "Mr. Moody, are you not a citizen of heaven?" To which the evangelist replied, "Yes, madam, I am a citizen of heaven, but as of now I vote in Cook County, Illinois."

Moody understood the double obligation of Christians to live out our faith in both the sacred and secular realms. That includes bringing to bear the overall moral imperatives of the Christian ethic to every part of the secular world, including, in this case, the problem of "big" government.

Let me make some initial disclaimers. I do not for a moment believe in unlimited power for the federal government or for any other agency of government, state or local. I support the manifold limits upon state power written into the

Constitution and the Bill of Rights. I am deeply concerned about any attempt to undermine those limitations.

I believe also that local authorities should handle purely local problems, so that lawmaking and regulation remain as close to the people as possible. One must, however, distinguish between local problems and those that impinge upon people far beyond the local limits. Environmental pollution is one example of something that seriously threatens us all. It is not a "local" problem.

One other disclaimer. I recognize the difficulties and defects in the American democratic process. We need to work to correct and reform those shortcomings, but I recall the oft-quoted words: "Democracy is about the worst system of government one can imagine—until you compare it with the alternatives."

What does the Christian faith say about big government? For one thing, our faith says a vigorous "yes" to the basic individual rights enshrined in the constitutional Bill of Rights. Freedom of religion, separation of church and state, freedom of speech, press, and assembly—there should be no compromise in these areas. Given the concern of Jesus for the integrity and value of each human individual, the Christian has a mandate to help safeguard those liberties that make each person's life worth living. It amazes me that many of those who vociferously declaim against big government's supposed infringements on their own freedoms are at the same time, paradoxically, in the forefront of those who would erode the rights of people who disagree with them. Continued efforts to blur the demarcation between church and state are a case in point. So, too, is the organized effort to attach an amendment to the Constitution that would declare our multi-faith nation a "Christian" state, whatever that term may mean in that context.

The French philosopher Voltaire was not himself an orthodox Christian, but he spoke words that Christians can surely affirm when he said, "I do not agree with a word you say, but I would defend to the death your right to say it." Those sentiments are not only democratic in the full American sense, they are consonant with Christian moral convictions.

I would suggest another Christian perspective that is important in the area of government. Though the constitutional documents are not written in theological language, they clearly demonstrate that the Founding Fathers were well aware of the biblical doctrine that all human beings are flawed by sin. They devised a political system, unique in its day, that set out a division of powers among the three

branches of government—executive, legislative, and judicial. They also included in the structure of government a complex system of checks and balances between and among those branches. The system is an explicit recognition of the conviction that no individual or group can ever be trusted with unlimited power. Plato's myth of an idyllic state ruled by incorruptible philosopher-kings is just that—a myth. No one is incorruptible.

Thus far, my attempt to apply Christian perspectives to the problem of big government has emphasized important limitations on government power: civil rights, separation of powers, and checks and balances. I hold these limitations to be of vital importance, and I recommend that my friends on the so-called Radical Right reflect seriously and gratefully about these protections of their own individual liberties.

I also have, however, positive words to say about big government. The first and simplest thing is that, given the size, geographically and population-wise, of a country like the United States, no alternative to big government is actually available. Ours is an incredibly complex society, economically, socially, and in every other aspect. Moreover, we are inescapably part of a world community in which national boundaries can no longer limit the effect of developments. What happens on the Wall Street stock market, for instance, affects millions of people everywhere. If television news reports a devaluation of the Brazilian currency, the shock waves reverberate in national economics around the world. If the East Asian financial structures collapse or if violence or anarchy erupts in Eastern Europe, the safety, jobs, and savings of millions of ordinary citizens in virtually every country in the world are threatened. No wonder that in such situations there are always calls for urgent national and international action to avert a worsening crisis. No "little" government could possibly act effectively in these circumstances.

Of course, as I have already said, many problems require only local action or perhaps no governmental action at all. These relatively minor difficulties, however, fade into insignificance beside the manifold interrelationships and crises of an intricately interdependent national and global society, requiring swift and massive action by big governments.

To look at the current human situation and the society in which we operate is to become increasingly aware of a pervasive factor: the relative helplessness or powerlessness of the individual citizen. That helplessness is not primarily the result

of government interference but a function of the complex and impersonal forces that impinge upon every individual's personhood and independence.

I can call up only representative examples here, and I continue to choose them from the economic realm. My personal financial situation is in many ways beyond my control. True, many people can prepare themselves for a job or a profession, work hard, and perhaps progress toward a decent salary, enabling them to plan for their futures. It is still possible for a relatively few individual entrepreneurs, blessed with talent and a considerable amount of luck, to become millionaires without benefit of the popular television quiz program. In the larger sense, however, we are all at the mercy of a complex, worldwide macroeconomic system. National and international economic booms, recessions, and depressions arrive, and we have not the slightest personal influence over them. The Japanese economy falters, and workers in Peoria lose their jobs. The dollar, the pound, or the yen fluctuates, and our stock market investments, if we are able to afford any, fluctuate in responding but unpredictable rhythms.

It is no wonder that economics has been dubbed the "dismal science." It seeks to chart a dangerous minefield. Some of my conservative friends argue for a stringent "laissez-faire" government policy in this area. I have an intelligent friend who strongly resents the power of the Federal Reserve Bank to control interest rates. These people seem to believe in some sort of "Unseen Hand" that will work everything out for most of us happily and fairly, so long as the government keeps its hands off the nation's and the world's economy. I see little evidence of the working of that Hand, and, taking into account the inherent greed and sinfulness of humanity, I have little confidence in it. One thing of which I am fairly certain is that if an "Unseen Hand" does exist, it is not God's hand. Given the widespread poverty and suffering of millions of our fellow humans, it is much more likely to be a satanic hand.

I am no economist, and I can speak with no authority in that specialized field. I cannot presume to prescribe detailed economic policies for the nation. I think, however, that I do reflect the situation of the average citizen when I say that when it comes to the larger economic situation, I feel powerless. The ordinary person, working hard to provide support and security for a family, requires some protection against the machinations of corporate and international finance—machinations he or she cannot control, largely is not aware of, and could not understand even if that

awareness were possible. The increasingly complex relationship of national and international economies only underlines my helplessness. The economic world is more and more controlled and influenced by giant multinational corporations, transcending national boundaries. Mergers and takeovers are in every day's financial headlines. I, as an individual, have no control or influence over those developments. Even one of the most successful modern entrepreneurs and currency speculators, George Soros, has written of his growing fears of what the almost totally unregulated international currency market can do to the average American.

Where else are we ordinary people to turn but to the power of a democratic government, responding to the needs and desires of its people?

I have said that I, as an individual, am powerless in this situation. But that is a relative judgment. I am not nearly so helpless as many millions of my fellow citizens. I am a retired university professor. I have a reasonable retirement pension, social security (a "big government" achievement), medical insurance, and some savings. My situation is relatively secure. I am disturbed by the fact that millions of my fellow Americans, not to mention untold multitudes in the rest of the world, have no such security.

I do not think I am someone who is simply envious of others who have more material things than I have. I do not resent the self-made millionaire who buys himself a Rolls Royce or a Jaguar, plus a mansion on the beach. I would not take that right away from him. I do wonder sometimes why an individual needs not one luxury car but five, and not one mansion but several. How much does it take in material goods to buy comfort and happiness?

As a Christian, I feel shame that in the most prosperous country in the world there are still millions of human beings who do not enjoy a half-decent standard of living. In an era of unprecedented prosperity, the statistics show that the gap between rich and poor has been growing steadily larger.

My more conservative friends tell me that these poverty-stricken people have only themselves to blame. They are lazy, criminal, unambitious, and immoral. As a firm believer in the universality of human sin I must agree that that judgment is probably accurate about many of these people, though in this sense their basic problem is no different from mine. But I also know that many of these unfortunates suffer from factors over which they have no control. They are the tragically disadvantaged of our world. Their fate was to be born in certain situations: race,

gender, family poverty, environment, mental or physical disability, which they did not choose and cannot change. They started the race of life fifty or a hundred yards behind the starting line, and it ill behooves those of us who have been more fortunate to condemn them because they never caught up.

All of this is to say that in our complex world I see a democratic government as the prime protector of the powerless and the disadvantaged in our society. My modest charitable contributions will, I hope, help, but I know they are minor in the total context. What the powerless and the helpless in our society need is not only Christian charity, admirable as that is, but concrete legal and governmental action to help reshape the total social picture toward an appropriate focus on "justice for all."

Here we would do well to learn some history lessons. When the Radical Right declaims against "big government," they need to remember our past. If it had not been for the actions of a big federal government, human slavery might have continued to exist in this country for decades. If it had not been for big government intervention, there would never have been a federal banking system, and in the 1930s hundreds of local banks would have closed their doors, and the savings of millions would have been decimated. It was big government that intervened to stop the building of ever more trusts and cartels, designed to exploit American consumers. Had not a visionary American president with a big government behind him—sometimes using less than orthodox methods—understood the ultimate threat of Hitler, western Europe and perhaps the world might now be dominated by Nazi tyranny. Children in the United States might still be working in mines and factories, laborers might still be toiling sixty or seventy hours a week, and men and women might still be doing their work in criminally unsafe conditions had it not been for government intervention. African-Americans might still be denied entrance to restaurants, theaters, hotels, and universities in the United States had not government stepped in. These are incontrovertible lessons of history.

None of these processes were perfect or without problems. The government has not always been on the side of the powerless. Many legitimate grounds for criticism of government policies exist, and I join in those criticisms. The federal government is a giant bureaucracy, and inherent weaknesses are part of any bureaucracy, even that of a multinational private corporation. Waste and inefficiency are often rife. Indeed, if you want an example of bureaucratic corruption,

take a look at many local school boards. Still, my overall summary view is that democratic government has proved itself the prime defense of the helpless.

What does all this mean for the Christian, striving conscientiously to be a good citizen in today's America? I think it means a great deal. No serious reader of the Scriptures can doubt the compassion and concern of God through his son, Jesus Christ, for the poor, the weak, and the powerless in every society. We tap ancient Hebrew wisdom when we take note of the words of the psalmist, "Defend the poor and fatherless; do justice to the afflicted and needy" (Ps 82:3). We need to hear again the most forthright and fiery of Old Testament prophets, Amos, calling down terrible judgment upon the society of his day. Why? Hear Amos thunder, "forasmuch as your treading is upon the poor, and you take from him burdens of wheat: you have built houses of hewn stone, but you shall not dwell in them; you have planted pleasant vineyards, but you shall drink no wine of them" (Amos 5:11).

No one can misunderstand the import of the words of Jesus: "Insomuch as you have done it unto one of the least of these my brethren, you have done it unto me" (Matt 25:40) The cup of cold water we give to a thirsty human being is a concrete response to the Master's command. But if all we do is give a cup of water, that man or woman will be thirsty again in a few hours. To do justice and seek righteousness is to do whatever we can with the tools at our command, not just to feed and clothe the poor but to change social structures and conditions. The poor will go on being poor, and the oppressed will go on being oppressed, unless we act to provide a level playing field and a genuine equality of opportunity. In this complex world it is the government that offers the best means to achieve those ends.

I am not a Utopian. I do not envision a human world without pain, suffering, poverty, or injustice. Neither am I an idealist when it comes to government. Government is an all-too-human institution, subject to all the limitations implied by that description. I foresee no perfect political party, president, Congress, or Supreme Court. Those options are not on offer, but these realistic recognitions do not absolve me from my Christian responsibilities. The scabs and sores of our society need healing. I am constrained by my Christian faith to give a cup of cold water, again and again, but my Christian duty reaches beyond that. I must do what I can, and wherever I can, to make the overall societal situation at least a bit better.

When I—a relatively powerless individual in a complicated world—look at my realistic options, one thing seems clear. My most effective avenue of action is

the exercise of my rights and privileges as a democratic citizen. Along with others I can make my voice heard in a free, representative government—one with built-in protections for individual rights and prescribed processes to guard against the usurpation of power by any group.

It is in this sense, with all reasonable reservations and disclaimers, that I say my modest "hurrah" for big government.

<h1 style="text-align:center">18</h1>

Wanted: A Public Philosophy

(*This article first appeared in* Christian Ethics Today.)

During 1963 and 1964 I spent much of my time in an in-depth study of the career of Walter Lippmann, the political columnist and philosopher. The result was a book called *Twentieth Century Pilgrimage: Walter Lippmann and the Public Philosophy*. The book, I must confess, made hardly a ripple in the wide sea of political thought.

Lippmann is remembered today primarily as an influential syndicated newspaper columnist. Indeed, at one point his status inspired a famous New Yorker cartoon, depicting two dowagers at the breakfast table on a New York commuter train. One lady says to the other, "Just a cup of coffee and Walter Lippmann. That's all I need for breakfast." But Lippmann was respected by more than commuters. When he visited London, he was received by Winston Churchill. Two lengthy interviews with Nikita Khrushchev, the Russian leader, were internationally televised and resulted in a best-selling book. And shortly after John F. Kennedy was elected president, he visited Lippmann for a long session of political advice and counsel.

Lippmann, however, was much more than a widely read political pundit. Across his half-century career he produced a series of thoughtful books. His 1922 work called *Public Opinion* is still ranked as a classic in its field. The most important of his books, setting out his mature and considered views, was a slim volume called *The Public Philosophy* that appeared in 1955.

In recent days I have gone back to that seminal publication and have found it even more relevant and insightful than when I first read it. Lippmann's prophecies have been largely fulfilled, and his analysis remains pertinent, more than forty years later.

What problems disturbed Lippmann? He saw the recent history of Western society as drastic evidence of dangerous political decay. Possessing the greatest accumulation of technological power and potential the world has ever known, victorious in battle in World War II (and now in the Cold War) over all enemies, verbally committed to high ideals and noble purposes, the democratic nations have still failed by and large to achieve the kind of society expected by their people and demanded by the times.

The trends Lippmann described in 1955 have become more pronounced in the years since. Today we are an economically prosperous society; yet there are potentially convulsive problems lurking below the political surface. We are a nation of conflicting pressure groups in constant struggle with one another. Of course, in one sense it has always been so. The difference today is that many of these pressure groups—ethnic, economic, social—seem gradually to be giving up on the prescribed democratic means of change. We condemn the terrorist methods of Palestinian guerrillas or Algerian rebels; yet we are nourishing within our own boundaries a situation in which our rapidly expanding underclass—people who no longer feel they have a stake in the maintenance of a democratic society—increasingly are led to resort to antidemocratic tactics. Force begets force, and a democratic society threatened by internal convulsion is steadily tempted to abandon its own principles and meet brute power with even greater power.

How has this happened? Why does an America committed to peace and freedom now have to deal with anarchic militia groups who blow up buildings in Oklahoma City? Why must we face lawless and destructive uprisings of the economically and socially depressed classes in our cities? Why are so many inner city areas now "no-go" areas for even the appointed forces of the law? Why does the gap between the rich and the poor grow steadily larger?

The situation is certainly not helped by a significant warping of the original theory of rule by democratically elected representatives. The founders and most of the early leaders of the American republic subscribed to the concept set out most clearly by the English parliamentarian Edmund Burke. Government was to be

administered by representatives elected by the people in a system that was opti-
mistically expected to place in office the most capable and thoughtful leaders of
the nation. These representatives were expected to use their own wisdom and conscientious judgment to put legislation into place. In our revolutionary information
and media age, that theory has devolved in practice into a system that favors the
election of those candidates with the most money to spend and the most effective
"spin doctors." Once in office, these elected officials are prisoners of volatile and
rapidly changing public opinion, expected not to exercise any independent judgment but to conform to the wishes of 51percent of their constituents. The
spectacle of an American president with three television sets in the Oval office, so
that he could be up-to-date instantly on the opinion polls of all three major television networks, is a sad commentary on the present system. Rubber stamp
representative government, responding to a public opinion manipulated by skillful
use of half-truths and inadequate, sensationalized media exposure, can rapidly
degenerate into the rule of the mob.

Walter Lippmann, however, was concerned with more basic problems than
these largely technical ones. He believed that a central clue to our difficulty lies in
the progressive loss of what he called the "public philosophy" or the "tradition of
civility"—a body of knowledge and understanding slowly and painfully arrived at
over more than twenty centuries of Western thought and experience. Within this
overall loss the most serious problem is the loss of any generally accepted moral
standard.

The inescapable fact is that nowadays many people, perhaps most, do not
actually believe in universal moral rules. Every situation in which people find
themselves appears to be different, and every moral decision they make is surrounded by a complex, compromising halo of extenuating circumstance. "Thou
shalt not steal"—fine, but perhaps if you had a violent father, or a drunken mother,
a lousy education, and the gene for criminality, then stealing would be, if not
excusable, then at least not really your fault. Certainly the kind of theft that
involves intricate corporate legal maneuvers or political chicanery isn't really covered by that injunction. And the average gland-crazed teenager would probably
think "Thou shalt not commit adultery" a pretty stupid rule when he has been
brainwashed by the culture to believe that every woman, married or not, is panting
for sex and eagerly awaiting his virile advances.

Brian Appleyard, an astute British critic of the contemporary scene, has recently written, "Modern morals, if any, tend to be entirely subjective and limited only at the outermost margins by the objective reality of the existence of other people" (*The Times*, London [4 January 1998]).

Lippmann foresaw this moral anarchy almost half a century ago. Increasingly over the last few decades we have seen the rise of the cult of the individual. In our laudable exaltation of the ideal of individual freedom, we have lost sight of the equally important ideal of individual and social responsibility. An overarching and generally agreed sense of community morality has been replaced by an anarchic ethic that makes morality for many purely a matter of individual preference. Each individual is the final judge of right and wrong. What's "good for me," a standard largely determined by the degree of personal pleasure or material gain, is somehow transmuted into what is good for all. The individual reigns as moral king.

The problem with this kind of individualistic ethic is that (with my sincere apologies to the human race, of which I am most definitely a part) most individuals are narrow-minded and shortsighted. The tradition of general moral rules, affecting everyone's behavior, incorporates spiritual insight and wisdom, hard earned and long tested. These precepts, of which a prime example is the Ten Commandments, are based on the impact of individuals in the wider realm. In the Old Testament, Jehovah saw the entire history of the people of Israel as dependent on their general obedience to moral law. And in the end Jehovah was right. The Jewish and later the Christian view triumphed and eventually formed a civilization—not perfect, by any means—but one of unparalleled freedom, wealth, and creativity. It is therefore simply moral madness to dump the accumulated religious and ethical wisdom of the centuries.

What is the root cause of this contemporary moral madness? Lippmann believed that it arises out of the fact that modern man has been systematically conditioned to believe that reliable knowledge can only arise out of that which can be sensibly experienced and mathematically verified. Blithely casting aside the long history of the struggle for a humanizing civilization, today's individual is effectively cut off from the past, thereby losing touch with the truth that teaches the necessity for the subjugation of a person's first nature—existence in self-centered barbarism—to the moral demands of his second nature—the realm of essence and ultimate reality.

As a result, for many today there is no room for a supremely important structure of "oughtness," a final moral standard by which all human actions are judged. No such standard can arise out of or be derived from the ambiguous earth-bound flow of human existence, flawed as it is by its concentration on the pleasure, power, and material gain of the individual. What Confucius called the "mandate of heaven" can only be glimpsed in our contact with the reality of essence, a level of being outside of ordinary human existence—outside our space-time box. For centuries mankind's spiritual and philosophic geniuses have sought to discover and establish a moral standard that requires that each individual's actions must be ethically measured, not only the consequences for the individual, but also by the effect upon others in the total community of which we are inescapably a part. Without such a standard we are condemned to live in a largely amoral world in which it is every person for himself herself and the devil take the hindmost. Thomas Hobbes's ghastly vision of a society in which every person is at war with every other person is the depressing result.

The centuries-long search for this ultimate standard is what Lippmann meant by the "traditions of civility." He believed, as I do, that such values as truth, beauty, and love are not pathetic phantasms of the human imagination but final constituents of moral reality. Through our human search (and for the Christian, as we shall see in a moment, through the graceful revelation of God in Christ) we have discovered intimations of that realm of essence. It is imperative that we do not discard or disregard that most significant achievement of the human pilgrimage.

True, these moral values do not supply us with a legalistic set of rules, automatically applicable to every human situation. Created as free moral agents, we have the responsibility of moral struggle as we attempt, always in the light and judgment of those values, to work out decisions in the ambiguity of existence. In many cases, given the nature of an imperfect and sinful world, we can only hope to achieve that which is "more right" under the circumstances. But what is "more right" must always be measured by essential and final moral standards.

Where does the faithful Christian believer stand in this situation? As Christians, we believe that we have been transformed by the grace of God into "new beings," "born-again" men and women. We do not kid ourselves that this means we are ethically perfect and without sin. In fact, we are more conscious of our sin and moral failure than ever before. But in our encounter with the

Christ-event we have been brought face to face with the ultimate ethic of perfect love. Jesus did not discard or ignore the Old Testament Law—the Ten Commandments—but he absorbed those commandments into a deeper and far more demanding ethic, most succinctly set out in the Sermon on the Mount.

An essential part of our Christian calling is to proclaim that perfect-love ethic to the world around us and to try to live it out. But we must also realize that without the pre-conditions of Christian conversion and commitment, that ethic never makes sense to the world at large. Today we live in a multicultural, multireligious society. Without in any way neglecting our evangelistic imperative, we must also lend our efforts to the establishment and maintenance of a society in which such minimal standards as justice, honesty, fairness, integrity, and respect for human beings as valuable entities, each in his or her own right, are recognized and adhered to.

It is a testimony to the validity of the realm of moral essence that the world's great religions and most of the world's greatest philosophers have centered upon the struggle to find some moral absolute. Even the sincere secular humanist seeks some ultimate moral meaning in the universe. Lippmann, though not himself a professing Christian, repeatedly picked out the Christian Church through the ages as the single most powerful testimony to the "tradition of civility." Speaking in 1938 to an Salvation Army dinner in New York, Lippman said, "The final faith by which all human philosophies must be tested, the touchstone of all party creeds, all politics of state, all relations among men, the inner nucleus of the universal conscience, is in possession of the Salvation Army."

Lippmann's recognition, which I share, places a heavy responsibility on the modern Christian community. It is an essential part of our mission to support and uphold those "traditions of civility" that undergird a public philosophy. To do so is not to be disloyal to our faith. Far from it. Jesus certainly demands from us in the realm of ethics more than justice, fairness, honesty, and integrity. He demands perfect love, which transcends all of these lesser values. However, it is important to remember that he never demands less than justice, fairness, honesty, and integrity in our every action. We betray him when we settle for anything less.

I believe with all my heart that God is concerned about every Christian believer, but I am constrained to believe by the nature of whom I worship that God is deeply concerned about every little human entity everywhere. I believe God's

love and compassion reach out to a starving Arab child, to a suffering Chinese dissident, to a morally and educationally deprived teenager in an American urban ghetto, and to an ordinary citizen cheated and deprived by a greedy, profit-driven business executive. If God cares, then so must I. My care must be translated into a struggle to change the situation as much as I can and at least to bring others closer to those moral standards that should be acknowledged by the whole society.

Lippmann believed, as I do, that no free and democratic—no "good" human society, can long endure without a "mandate from heaven." When our Founding Fathers in America incorporated into the Declaration of Independence the phrase "All men are created equal," they acknowledged that the right of every human being to life, liberty, and the pursuit of happiness is a God-given, natural right. I do not mean to say that any earthly government is a reflection of the will of God. I do not believe in the "divine right of kings"; neither do I believe in the "divine right of America." What I do believe is that a good government and a good society is one that takes seriously an overarching structure of right and wrong and is not reluctant to have its actions measured by that standard. This applies to every part of that government, from its elected president on down to the humblest citizen.

Human equality under law and the consequent right to justice can never be demonstrated in the laboratory or by mathematical calculations. Values such as honesty, faithfulness, and integrity can never be established by public opinion polls. These values are derived from the realm of essence. They are "there." In Christian terms they are God-given. The truth of that proposition is our legacy of centuries of human struggle, our "traditions of civility," our "mandate from heaven."

I believe that the greatest moral and ethical challenge of our day is not that of any particular and specific moral issue or evil, important as they may be. Our challenge is to reestablish, reinforce, and undergird the public philosophy. That task cannot be accomplished by force or by direction from the "powers that be" in earthly terms. No amendment to the United States Constitution declaring us to be a "Christian" nation will make one whit of difference. The task can only be accomplished by people of faith and good will—politicians, educators, business men and women, working people, all of us—sounding out loud and clear our testimony and our witness.

Christians, as always, have a major role to play. We are called to that task as surely as any minister or missionary is called to his or her vocation. To fail to

respond to that challenge in the pulpit or in the pew, to shrug off its imperative importance, is in the deepest and most meaningful sense a denial of our faith.

III

19

CREDO

An individual's autobiography is of primary interest only to the person who writes it. Any person's life story is an odyssey. Although relatively inconsequential in the total scheme of things, it is a matter of vital concern to the man or woman it portrays. If that life has a significant spiritual dimension, the odyssey can become a pilgrimage—a lifelong search for ultimate truth and reality. From this perspective, the tale may possibly be of interest to others engaged in the same sort of spiritual adventure.

My own pilgrimage has now gone on for over seventy-seven years. In that trek I have found no permanent resting place—no finality that satisfies me. The search goes on. Limited as we are by our humanness and our sinfulness, we can never hope to arrive at an incontrovertible point at which we can say with assurance, "This is it. I have found the answer." Life in my experience is a constant readjustment of ideas and convictions. Through my years I have gone on learning. When I was a pastor, I had a good doctor friend whom I often saw when I visited patients in the hospital. He was not a member of any church and was an avowed religious skeptic. When I passed him in the hospital corridor, he often called out to me, jocularly but with a hint of a barb, "Hi, parson. What do you know today—for sure?" I was never quite certain then, nor I am sure today, exactly how to answer him.

I am not the person I was fifty years ago. That is obviously true in a physical sense. Much of the hair on my head has disappeared. My hearing is artificially enhanced, and I have recently had cataract surgery to restore my eyesight to usable dimensions. But I have not only changed physically. Across that period of time I have changed markedly in spiritual and intellectual ways.

I do not believe all the things I once believed, and new concepts and understandings have replaced old ones in my mental and spiritual outlook. If the afterlife and heaven are what I hope they will be, my continuous process of learning and correction will go on until at last I see, not "as in a glass darkly," but "face to face." I shall finally know.

I became a Christian at the age of twenty-three. A year later I was ordained to the Christian ministry. Four years later I became a pastor, and ten years after that I entered upon doctoral study at university. That experience prepared me to teach at the university level, and I then became a university chaplain, a professor of religion, and, finally, a university administrator. Throughout all that period I have thought of myself primarily as a preacher, seeking to proclaim and explain the Christian gospel.

Obviously, I never quite settled down in a professional occupation. When my younger son was a student at Florida State University, he had trouble deciding on his academic major, changing his mind several times. When I gently reprimanded him about this, he replied, "Dad, you are the last person in the world to criticize me for that indecision. You never have been able to make up your mind what you really wanted to be."

My son was right. In addition to my professional career as preacher, pastor, teacher, and university official, I have also spent time across the years as a soft-drink vendor, a men's clothing salesman, a paid political campaign speaker, a dining room waiter, a radio newscaster, a business motivational speaker, a part-time speech advisor to a candidate for Texas governor, a soldier, and a writer. Along the way I have endured most of the experiences that many other human beings have encountered. Violent death, loss of loved ones, the collapse of a marriage, occasional betrayal by trusted friends, personal and professional rejection, failure to achieve treasured ambitions, physical pain and suffering—these have all been integral parts of my life story. Retirement adds a new perspective. I am dealing with the creeping intimations of age and the creaking of old bones.

I cannot say honestly that I regret any of this. Each event has helped me to understand myself a little better and also to empathize more accurately with the people and the world about me. Personal and spiritual growth for any of us are the products of accumulated experience. As we live, we grow, and hopefully in the process we become more sensitive human beings. At best, life events also help us to enlarge and deepen our spiritual understanding.

What have all these years taught me? In the preface to this volume I warned my readers that they would not find any unifying structure in the book, given the nature of its material. In looking back now, as my task of putting the book together comes to an end, I must modify that judgment. It seems to me that there are certain unifying themes that run throughout the articles and essays. Picking out those themes may be a useful way of summing up some of the basic facets of my own beliefs and convictions at this point in my life.

Underneath everything I have tried to say is, I think, a pervading conviction of the supreme importance of that indefinable and mysterious element in the Christian life—the grace of God. By grace I mean, as best I can understand it, the working and intervention of God in individual human lives and expressly in mine. I have said elsewhere in this volume that I cannot fully define grace. It is certainly not predictable. Just as clearly, it cannot be contracted or bargained for. It "just happens." Since the conviction of grace is dependent upon personal experience, my belief in this working of God is finally a mystical one. I plead guilty to being a "mystic" in this sense. That recognition, however, is consistent with my belief that the final basis of all valid religious faith is personal experience.

This emphasis on personal religious experience is essential to my understanding of the Christian faith. I fail to understand how any existential conviction of the truth of the faith can rest on anything else but experience. Walter Rauschenbusch, the great Baptist theologian of another generation, put it this way: "The Christian faith, as Baptists hold it, sets spiritual experience boldly to the front as the one great thing in religion." This is, frankly, what has constrained me to remain a Baptist across all the years when many of my respected friends moved to other denominations. Baptists began with a courageous defense of the right of every human being to work out his or her own religious faith on the basis of his or her own experience and understanding of what the Bible means. Surrendering that right is, it seems to me, giving up the essence of faith. Without personal religious experience to undergird doctrine, the faith becomes little more than the dry and lifeless recitation of creeds or catechisms. I cannot understand how anyone who has experienced in life the working of the grace of God can deny it, and I cannot believe that anyone who has never experienced that working can comprehend it.

Certainly, no one person's spiritual experience is final or definitive. As Christians we are members of a community of faith. The input of the wider

Christian community is essential for correction, but the individual believer must make the ultimate decision, if it is to have validity. This leads me to another basic theme that I discern as underlying my writings. It is not a pleasant theme, but I think it is inescapable. I refer to the recognition that human limitation and sin impact everything we say, do, and believe.

I have said elsewhere in this material that I am not a Calvinist, in the strict interpretation of that term. I do not believe that any human being is totally bad, but I do believe that every person, including myself, is a complex mixture of good and evil. No human activity is untouched by what Reinhold Niebuhr called "the greasy thumbprint" of sin. We are all a mixture of lust and love, love and hate, egotism and altruism, idealism and hard self-centered practicality. This recognition of reality should produce in each of us the prime Christian virtue of humility. Humility is an honest recognition of our own fallibility and innate corruptibility. This recognition saves us from the sin of what I have called religious "imperialism"—the overriding certainty that we are completely right whereas all others are wrong. I have personally tried never to go into the pulpit and preach anything I believed to be wrong or in error, but I have also felt that I was always susceptible to correction and further instruction. Christian growth is a continuous process of change, hopefully for the better.

It is essential to remember that no human being and no human institution can escape the contagion of sin and evil. When I entered the Christian ministry and became a pastor as a young man, I did so with enthusiasm and a certain degree of naivete. Surely, I thought, the fraternity of men and women dedicated to the "high calling" of Christian service will be a sort of Utopian moral community, marked by consecrated unselfishness and sacrificial labor for the kingdom of God. Because I was the pastor of a large church, I rapidly entered into positions of leadership in my denomination. I did find myself in association with hundreds of good men and women, trying their best to do their Christian tasks, but I also discovered that the malignant strains of personal ambition and the lust for power were not foreign to the community of Christian leadership. Later, when I left the pastorate and became a university professor, I carried with me yet again a bit of that same naivete and unrealistic expectation. Surely, I thought, the community of scholars, dedicated seekers of the truth in every intellectual area, will be relatively free from that "greasy thumbprint." Again I was doomed to disappointment. For a time in

my university career I was chairman of the Faculty Senate, the representative body of university professors in their relationship with the administration and the institution as a whole. My experience there led me to say, hyperbolically and tongue-in-cheek, that the Faculty Senate was a prime laboratory for the study of original sin and total depravity. Thus, out of the hard data of my own experience and my association with some of the "brightest and best" human institutions, I draw my firm conclusion that the harsh reality of human sin is an indispensable element in the construction of any thinking person's faith.

Yet another theme that runs through these articles, especially those that try to address specific ethical problems, is the conviction that everyday life is a constant struggle between the perfectionist stance of Christian love and the hard realities of the social, political, and economic conditions of the world around us. I have grudgingly had to admit that crusades for the perfect love-ethic of Jesus are not strikingly effective in the real world. Ethics in that world is a perpetual process of compromise. An unconverted world does not respond to cries for perfection, however eloquently and passionately those pleas are made. One must constantly settle for second-best. I have had to make my peace with the realization that ethical and moral progress consists not just in adamantly contending for the perfect, but often of settling for the "most-right" in a particular situation. I have had to admit that to achieve a little bit of progress toward a more loving, just, and equable world is better than to hold out for perfection and achieve nothing. To admit this is to take an humbler, more realistic attitude toward the world, but it is ultimately the attitude we must adopt. The world around us is not ideal and will never be. That does not excuse us from trying our best, as Christians, to make it measurably better.

The beliefs I have outlined here, important as I think they are, must be set in context in a total confession of faith. The ultimate character of one's religious commitment is largely determined by the choice of a central point of reference around which all subsidiary beliefs are arranged and measured. One thing must be most important, and all else must cohere with that central affirmation.

Some Christians opt to make the institutional church the center of their faith. They are loyal in their attendance and participation, and the church—its architecture, its music, the quality of its preaching, the acceptability of its liturgy, the scope of its activities—is of prime importance. Some go further and make the institutional church the final arbiter of doctrine and belief. Whatever the leaders of

their denomination say is orthodox, and they accept that as fact. Their final bastion of faith is the human church.

I must make a distinction here for the sake of clarity. The New Testament has much to say about the "church" and certainly does not denigrate its importance, but the prime scriptural definition of "church" is the Body of Christ, a mystical and supernatural concept. I distinguish here between that biblical understanding and the human ecclesiastical institution by capitalizing "Church" as the Body of Christ. From this perspective the Church cannot be totally identified with the church. The church, however high its motives and doctrines, is a human institution. As such, it is subject to the same kind of fallibility and imperfection as every other human construct. The church too often succumbs to the lure of materialism. It sometimes excludes individuals from its fellowship whom Christ would clearly accept. It tolerates and even sometimes exalts to positions of leadership people whose Christian commitment is ambiguous at best and whose motives are susceptible to legitimate suspicion. Every faithful Christian worker is painfully aware of the existence of the Church within the church.

I cannot organize my faith around any human institution, even the church. Though I cherish and support my church, I am much too aware through my own experience of its weaknesses. Though I respect many Catholic beliefs, I am not a Roman Catholic because, among other things, I cannot accept the concept of papal infallibility in matters of faith and practice. Similarly, I cannot give final authority to any one or any group of denominational leaders, or to the decisions of an assembly of people, adopted by a show of hands. Truth cannot be determined by majority vote. The church is not the determinant of my faith.

Many other Christians, especially within my own denominational tradition, elevate the Scriptures to the place of centrality. Here I must be especially careful, lest I be misunderstood. I am a biblical Christian, though some of my more fundamentalist friends would dispute that. I accept the Scriptures as the written record of God's dealings with creation through the centuries. I turn to the Bible constantly for inspiration and understanding. I would not for a moment want to underestimate its importance for me and for the Christian community. I have spent much of my life studying and pondering the teachings of the written word, and that has never been a fruitless or unsatisfying endeavor.

Some Christians hold firmly to the idea that every word of the Scriptures was divinely shaped and dictated directly by God through the Holy Spirit. I do not believe that. Many individuals wrote the Bible across many centuries of human history. Parts of the Bible represent not simply the work of a single person but the collective memories of large groups of people. I believe that this writing was always and everywhere inevitably influenced and partially shaped by the cultural and historical context in which it was written. When we read biblical writings, we must always be aware of those influences. Our interpretation of the writings must always take into account those factors. We must also constantly be aware that our own understandings are shaped by our personal cultural and historical context.

Even if the literal interpreters of Scripture are correct, they are left with a further problem. The Bible is written in human language, and language is an integral part of our own limitation. I have several times in this material used the metaphor of a time-space box. We are imprisoned within that box in our human existence, and every part of our experience, including our language, is made fallible and imperfect by those space-time dimensions. We think in terms of human understanding, but God's ultimate truth comes from outside the box. We can never totally comprehend it, and we are certainly not entitled to make our individual interpretations the final touchstone of religious faith.

I believe that God overshadowed the writing of the Scriptures but not to the extent of destroying the humanity and freedom of the writers. God and God's truth cannot be totally equated with the Bible. It is tragically possible to become a "Bibliolater," a worshiper of the Bible in place of the living God. Adopting that stance, we abandon the primary Christian virtue of humility and seek to make ourselves "popes," infallible dictators of what is religiously true or false That is the height of what the ancient Greeks called hubris, the greatest of sins against the gods.

If not the church and not the Bible, what then is the central stone in the arch of my own Christian faith? Here, in order to make sense of my answer to that question, I must digress to fill in some important personal background.

Throughout most of my life I have been an ardent lover of theater—not the cinema with its flickering screens, but the "on the boards" experience of living theater. At an early age I even had vague dreams of becoming a professional actor. Though my subsequent career did not go in that direction, I retained my intense

avocational interest, and I have spent much of my life, in a secondary sense, as an amateur actor and director in community and university theater. My experiences in the theater have been high points in my personal life.

In Britain there is a long-running radio program called "Desert Island Discs." Celebrities are invited on to the program and are asked to choose what books and musical recordings they would take with them if they knew they were going to be cast away on a desert island for many years. Their choices are interesting, but to me the most interesting thing is that they are restricted in their choice of books. They are told that they can take with them a copy of the Bible and a volume of the collected works of William Shakespeare. Their other choices must be in addition to those.

Why those two? The inclusion of the Bible is obvious, but why Shakespeare? Is it because, more so than any other Western writer, he has plumbed the depths in the interpretation of the human character and the human situation? Aristotle, the Greek philosopher, wrote that the ideal theatrical experience was one that he called "catharsis"—a sort of emptying out of the clogged human arteries of experience and an emotional "cleansing." Living in London, the theatrical capital of the world, I have been privileged to watch many of the finest performances of great theatrical artists. Seeing Laurence Olivier in "Richard III" and "Macbeth," John Gielgud in "The Tempest," and Alec Guinness in almost anything, I have discovered what Aristotle meant. The theatrical experience can lead us into an understanding of the human condition, perhaps as no other artistic experience can. I have learned much from the theater and from the writings of men like Shakespeare.

Years ago, in the pursuit of my theatrical avocation, I was cast in a minor supporting role in a play in the University Theater at Florida State University. The play starred the visiting artist Dana Andrews, cinema idol of the 1940s and 1950s. Andrews, a handsome man with considerable talent as an actor, had had a highly successful movie career. That career was blighted and virtually brought to an end by chronic alcoholism. When I met him, he was in the twilight of his career. He was recovering from his addiction, largely through the help of his lovely and devoted wife.

A chance correlation in our backgrounds brought us together. Andrews was the son of a Texas Baptist preacher who had been, for several years, the pastor of

the First Baptist Church in Huntsville, Texas. I had filled the pulpit in Huntsville on numerous occasions. That common experience (Andrews had been a child while his father was pastor in Huntsville) provided the beginning of a friendship that lasted, through correspondence, until Andrews's death.

The last word I had from Dana was a Christmas note written a few months before his death. In his note he said, "As you know, I have been to the depths but have recovered. In some familiar old words, I was lost but now am found. As an actor almost all my life, I tend to see things from a theatrical perspective. I see myself as a bit player in an eternal drama in which God is both the author and the protagonist. Though I have had only a few lines in the play, those lines have been written and directed by a loving Father."

Since I shared with Dana his love of the theater, I think I understand what he was saying. It has great meaning for me, and it particularly helps to shape my understanding of the Bible. To me the Bible is the inspired record of a cosmic drama, stretching across the ages and into eternity. That drama begins for us with the creation stories in Genesis. I have little interest in arguments about the details of that story. Genesis was not written as a scientific account of the creation process. Had it been written in scientific and technological language, it would have been little more than gibberish to those who first heard or read it. Indeed, much of it would still be incomprehensible to modern men and women.

The creation stories are profound poems, celebrating the wondrous mystery of creation. The most important words in Genesis are its opening declaration: "In the beginning God created." That affirmation rescues us from a meaningless and chaotic physical universe, called into being only by some strange chance and rumbling along in its development without purpose. From this perspective life has no final meaning; we are helpless dots of matter, struggling futilely in a giant sea of ultimate nothingness. To believe in the Genesis creation account is to find basis for the declaration that every created human being is important in the ultimate scheme of things.

The Genesis account continues with the temptation story. It reaches into the depths of human experience with its record of initial innocence, confrontation with temptation, the misuse of the God-given capacity of free moral choice, and the inevitable consequences of moral disobedience. Adam is the Hebrew word for man, and Adam and Eve's experience is the universal one. My name is also Adam.

God chose to create human beings in the pattern of "his own image." The divine image is a complex one, involving many facets. It means that we have been given a mental capacity that, to a limited degree, mirrors what I have elsewhere called the "Divine Sanity." The use of reason and logic is a prime constituent of humanness. Because we are creatures, and not creators, our use of reason will always be partial and incomplete, marred as always by sin; but to the extent that we follow accurately the paths of right thinking, we have one avenue that leads toward truth.

The divine image also includes as an essential element our ability to respond spiritually and aesthetically. We can, for instance, make musical instruments and use them to produce tunes and harmony. Beyond that we can compose not only simple "ditties," but complex operas, symphonies, and oratorios that reach out to the aesthetic and existential understanding of other people. We can create sculptures and paintings to which individuals respond with insight and imagination. We can develop not merely simple tools—a lever and a wheel—but incredibly complicated scientific and technological devices. Perhaps most importantly, we have developed the tools of language. We can verbally communicate, not only in the simplistic jargon of "Me—Tarzan; you—Jane," but in ways that enable philosophers, theologians, scientists, and artists to transmit the most involved and difficult ideas. We are able to resonate to the deeper meanings of terms such as truth and beauty. Most importantly, we are possessed of a hunger for spiritual understanding of the Ultimate. The continuous and unending search by men and women across the centuries for a contact with the Eternal bears vivid testimony to that human capacity. Had God not given us that facility, God, and all the surrounding reality, would be totally unapproachable and incomprehensible.

Finally, the divine image in us means that God in creation deliberately limited himself and his power over us by granting us human freedom—the ability to make meaningful moral choice. I say that God "limited" himself. This does not mean that there is anything God cannot do; rather it means that there are things God will not do. One of the things God will not do is override the moral and spiritual freedom of humans, even though the exercise of that freedom, as with Adam and Eve, may lead men and women into tragic rebellion against God's will.

Thus, the cosmic drama opens with scenes of creation, temptation, and what we have traditionally called the "fall of man." The Hebrew Scriptures that unfold

after those events are for me a God-guided record with two correlative themes. From the divine standpoint they are the record of God's patient and continuing effort to reveal his true nature and will, working with a particular group of people, the nation Israel. God's goal was the development of a godly and humane community, responsive to his leadership and serving as an example for the pagan world. Human pride, lust, and self-centeredness continually thwarted that purpose. This is the second major theme. Despite the fact that God raised up prophet after prophet to warn and correct Israel, the nation failed to respond in any consistent fashion. A recognition of this second theme should save us from the error of accepting human, and therefore sinful, actions on the part of the Israelites as abiding standards for our actions and attitudes. No single Old Testament figure, however admirable in many ways, can be accepted as an authoritative guide for us today.

All that has gone before in the Bible—creation, temptation, fall, the epic story of Israel—is but prologue. The drama rises to its climax in a unique and revolutionary happening, what we call today the Christ-event. All else in the Scripture is organized finally around that event and, therefore, all Scripture must be interpreted and understood in relation to that happening.

C. S. Lewis, the perceptive English teacher and theologian, is remembered by most people today for his masterful apologetic Christian writings. Lewis, however, was a man of manifold talents and in addition to religious works, he wrote a trilogy of novels that we would characterize today as "science-fiction." He allowed his imagination to set out stories of interplanetary travel and encounters with those we call extraterrestrial aliens. His stories were fanciful dreams, but he could not help but undergird them with a solid theological foundation, given his own background.

The first of his science-fiction novels is called *Out of the Silent Planet*. In the story, Lewis's hero, a scientist called Ransome, is transported to another planet (Venus, in the tale). There he encounters intelligent life forms. In fact, those life forms are far more intelligent and spiritually discerning that anything Ransome has experienced on earth. From them he learns that his own planet, Earth, is known as the "silent planet." It is so-called because, long ago, it rebelled against the creator God. Since that time its lines of communication with the rest of the universe have been severed. It is isolated and detached—silent.

Again and again God has sought to make vital contact with the inhabitants of Earth, to no lasting avail. His efforts are blocked, first, by the recalcitrance and self-centeredness of Earth's inhabitants, but also by the malignant workings of a supernatural power of evil, resisting every redemptive effort of the Almighty. At last God has determined to make one last effort. He will "invade" that silent planet in a way that it cannot help but confront. He will, in effect, go himself in a shape and form that Earth's inhabitants can recognize, and he will in concrete "flesh and blood" demonstrate and act out his loving purposes for his creatures. In Lewis's novel this is, of course, fiction, but it carries strong intimations of ultimate truth.

I have been using here a metaphor of the theater, which may not be as compelling to others as it is to me. But within that metaphor, the words of my friend, Dana Andrews, take on additional and, I think, profound meaning. Andrews saw himself as a "bit player" in a cosmic drama in which God was the author, director, and protagonist. Andrews's personal life was acted out and inevitably shaped by that drama.

I emphasize and identify with that. I see myself as a supporting player in that mighty drama, and I am confronted with the realization that my own life acts out, in minuscule form, that eternal plot. I came into being—I was "created"—at the moment of my birth. I have no knowledge or memory before that point. By whatever biological process, I was called into being out of nothingness. Thus, my own history mirrors the Genesis event. Like Adam and Eve, I walked for a time in a state of relative innocence, and like them also, I encountered temptation and succumbed to it. The desire to be more than I am, to aggrandize my own experience at the harmful expense of others, took control. I "fell" in the biblical sense, and the consequences for me, as for Adam and Eve, were catastrophic. I experienced guilt and alienation, and I was cast into a world of sin and oppression. My lot was not a happy one, though often I sought to convince myself that this was what existence was all about.

"Sin" is a controversial term, even for Christians. My own concept of the meaning of sin is that always and everywhere it involves concrete harm to other human beings. Some of my Christian friends argue that this is a deficient understanding of sin. Sin, they say, also involves a crime against God. The vertical understanding of sin is as important as the horizontal one. I totally agree, but I would go further to argue that there is no real transgression that does not involve

the misuse and mistreatment of other human beings. Again and again in the Old Testament, God raised up prophets to speak for him in denouncing the religious perversions of Israel. The sin of Israel was identified not primarily as the distortion of ritual, sacrifice, or religious practice, but as the oppression of individual human beings. Sin is against God, but that sin is concretely worked out in the misuse, manipulation, and corruption of other individuals. I understand that that is what Jesus meant when he put the two great commandments of the law—love of God and love of neighbor—on the same level.

Into my personal experience came, at a particular moment, an epochal and life-changing moment. I can only explain it in scriptural terms. The first words of the Gospel of John in the New Testament must be placed alongside those first words of Genesis. "In the beginning was the Word, and the Word was with God, and the Word was God" (John 1:1). The Word is central to all Christian understanding. "Word" is the vehicle of human understanding of God. In the beginning God "spoke" our human existence into being, and in the Christ-event God "spoke" the meaning of all existence into reality. In the unique and unrepeatable event of Jesus of Nazareth, God made his ultimate outreach to creation. That event was acted out in the historical occurrences of the life of Jesus—his birth, his life, his teaching, his death, and his resurrection. In that life God "emptied himself, and became obedient, event unto death." (Phil 13:1). God, for our sake, became flesh and blood. In that intervention into human life he challenged us finally to become what the Apostle Paul calls "perfect" (Phil 3:14); the better translation is "mature." In Christ we are called to become what God originally intended us to be—mature, fully human individuals, clearly reflecting the image of God in human clay.

Obviously, much of what I have said here, using my metaphor, will be unacceptable to many of my fundamentalist Christian friends. My understanding of the Scriptures will not meet their tests of orthodoxy. I am just as certain that what I have said will be characterized as mystical nonsense by many of my unbelieving, agnostic, or atheist associates. I can only plead that on the basis of my experience this is the only place at which I can at this moment take my stand.

I need to change my metaphor here from that of the theater to that of the legal courtroom. I would suppose that I might be called as a witness in a case. I would enter the courtroom, take the witness stand, and swear that what I had to

say would be "the truth, the whole truth, and nothing but the truth." At this point the prosecuting attorney would rise and begin to question me.

"You claim to be a Christian," he might ask. "What is it that you actually believe?"

"I am a Christian," I would say. "I base that affirmation on my own personal experience with the living Christ."

"So," the prosecuting attorney might say, "that is your faith. Do you have any solid evidence for that belief?"

Here, of course, I would be pressed into my own last defense. How could I answer, not only the attorney, but the myriad of scientists, rational thinkers, and philosophers who profoundly disagree with me? I think I could marshal a considerable amount of reasonable opinion, but I admit that on that basis alone I could make no final and altogether convincing case. My ultimate rationale must rest upon intensely personal experience. I would have to tell my story, and I do that now. This is my witness, my testimony, and the bedrock of my religious conviction. It is inevitably highly personal and must be judged as such.

My childhood and adolescent years were spent in a home environment that was nominally Christian and highly moral. I was taught from my earliest remembrance what was right and what was wrong, but my family at that point had no meaningful connection with the Christian church as such. The most important thing to do on most Sunday mornings was to drive the forty or so miles to a nearby town in order to gather at my grandfather's home with my father's extended family for a Sunday meal. Church attendance was much lower in the priority list.

My mother was a pious woman with a meaningful personal faith. She had been reared in a devout Disciples of Christ family. Though in her middle years she joined the Baptist church and served as a faithful teacher and worker in its ranks, I do not think she ever abandoned her basic "Campbellite" beliefs. I respected her for that.

My father grew up in a large, poverty-stricken, rural family in deep East Texas. His religious background was Primitive Baptist, and I think he waited through the first half of his life for some cataclysmic spiritual experience that would sweep him into the church. At any rate he was never a church member until he was over forty years old. When he did finally unite with the local Baptist church, he became a deacon and for more than thirty years was the teacher of a large men's Sunday

school class. When he died, the surviving aged members of his class stood together around his grave, bearing testimony to the influence of his life and teaching.

In this family context I spent my childhood and adolescent years with no involvement in church or, indeed, in religion. I was an "early achiever." In high school I had more recognition and honors than were good for me. When I graduated from Gladewater High School (Texas), I was president of my senior class and valedictorian. I had also been a successful high school debater. My debate coach, a mild-mannered English teacher, J. N. Shepherd, deeply influenced me. In addition to his teaching duties, he taught a high school boys' Sunday school class at the local First Christian Church. Under his influence I attended his class and eventually joined that church. I must sadly confess that that decision had no real spiritual meaning for me and little or no effect on my personal life and behavior. When I completed my high school work, I quickly drifted far away from any association with that church.

I completed high school in the spring of 1940. War was in the air, but it still seemed far away. I wanted very much to go on to a major university. My family was committed to providing higher education for my two younger sisters and me, but finances were a problem. I ended up enrolling in Kilgore Junior College, a small community college located only a few miles from where I lived. I could attend classes there and still stay at home, relieving the financial burden.

At Kilgore I continued my debating career. I was fortunate to have as a colleague a young man of remarkable talent, John Hill, who was to go on to become Attorney General and then Chief Justice of the Supreme Court of Texas. John and I journeyed to Charlotte, North Carolina, for the national junior college debating tournament and won the national championship. On our return we were feted, celebrated, and honored. It did no good at all for what was now my mammoth ego.

At the end of my freshman year at Kilgore, John left the school to go on to the University of Texas. Good luck gave me another competent debating colleague, Marvin Eichenroht, and at the national tournament that year, we managed to win the championship for a second time, a first in the records of that organization. I was still riding high. I had been president of my freshman class at Kilgore, and in my second year I was president of the student body. Along with my achievements, a darker side of my young life had emerged. In the rough-and-ready culture of the East Texas oil fields, many Kilgore students were part of a heavy drinking, sexually

promiscuous society. I did not distance myself from that culture but became an active part of it.

When I completed my community college work, I wanted to go on to the University of Texas where I would have joined my friend John Hill. Once again, finances reared its ugly head. My parents could see no way to underwrite my study at Texas University. My father had a passing acquaintance with the former governor of Texas, Pat Neff, who at that point was president of Baylor University, a Baptist institution in Waco, Texas. He made an appointment with Governor Neff, and I had an interview with him. Mr. Neff was a strong supporter of Baylor's outstanding intercollegiate debating program, and I emerged from that interview with a scholarship providing tuition, board, room, books, and laundry. I had no alternative. It was Baylor for me. In the summer of 1942 I reluctantly enrolled in the university.

The shadow of the war influenced everything young men of my age did in those days. In the first years of the war, college and university students had been automatically deferred from call-up to military service. We all knew that the situation would soon change. I wanted to get as much of my undergraduate education behind me as I could before I entered the military. I enrolled in Baylor at the beginning of the summer term, 1942, and continued to study there until I was called to military service. My previous successes continued at Baylor. With my debating colleague, Charles McGregor, we made the rounds of the somewhat abbreviated wartime schedule of intercollegiate debate tournaments and ended the season without a single defeat. I won a national oratorical contest sponsored by the U.S. Department of State and made my first journey outside the state of Texas to New York City to appear on a then-popular radio program, "Town Meeting of the Air." Without much difficulty I managed to chalk up high academic marks. Throughout this period I remained resistant and virtually impervious to the influence of that Christian university ethos, rarely if ever attending a church service. I viewed the religious fervor of many of my fellow students with amused disdain.

Military service was inevitable. I tried to complete as much of my undergraduate program as I could, but in the spring of 1943, with only one term of study remaining for my bachelor's degree, I had no time left. In order to maximize my opportunities in the military as much as possible, I volunteered for what was called the Army Specialized Training Program. I was promised that, after completion of the normal thirteen-week basic infantry training program, I would be sent back

to university somewhere for further training in some specialized area of military service.

So, in the summer of 1943, I found myself at Camp Roberts, California. It was 110 degrees in the shade and no shade for miles. Those first weeks of my life as a soldier were traumatic for me. I had never been an athlete and I was not well prepared physically for the tasks the army considered important in its basic training program. Whereas I had become accustomed to being first in almost every activity I undertook, I now found myself last or next to last in virtually every situation. In addition, I found the daily routine a thoroughly dehumanizing and degrading experience. No personal privacy was allowed, and our training activities were by and large boring and repetitive. I cannot blame the military for that. I understand that if they are to fulfill their mission, they must take ordinary soldiers and mold them into virtually unthinking, robotic, killing machines. I was not a religious person, but I did have genuine moral qualms about the rightness of killing other human beings, however justified the cause. Suffice it to say that at Camp Roberts that summer, I was not a "happy camper."

My personal situation was to worsen still further. All of my fellow trainees were volunteers for the same program in which I had enlisted. As we came into the last two weeks of our basic program, daily notices were posted on the company bulletin board, indicating where individuals were to be assigned at the end of their training. A large group was going to the University of Nebraska, another group to Tulane University in New Orleans. To my consternation, my name did not appear on any list.

I became anxious enough to make a trip to the Army Personnel Center to inquire about my situation. I was assigned for an interview with a bored, older major who obviously could not have cared less about my problems. He took a quick look at my records, lit another cigarette, and informed me, "Some army clerk has messed up your records. You will not be sent back to college when your finish your training here."

I could hardly believe my ears. "What's going to happen to me?" I asked.

His answer was brief and to the point. "When you complete your basic training, you will be given a ten-day furlough. You can go home."

"What then?" I asked.

"You will report back to Fort Ord, California. From there you will be sent to the South Pacific as a rifleman replacement."

My heart sank. In those days of the Pacific war, that sounded almost like a death sentence to me, but there was apparently nothing I could do.

I was desperate—so much so that, a few days later, I made one last despairing trip to the Personnel Center. They granted me another interview, this time with a debonair young captain who seemed much more concerned with me and my problems. But his initial verdict was the same.

"It's not your fault, but your records are in a mess. There is no way at this time that I can get you assigned to the college program."

He thought for a moment and then riffled through some papers on his desk.

"There is one remote possibility," he said. "I gather that you don't want to go to the South Pacific and that you would like the chance to spend at least another six months of training in the States before going overseas."

"Yes, sir," I said, with my heart in my mouth.

"Okay. If you will sign this paper, I can absolutely guarantee you that you will not be sent to the Pacific and that you will spend several more months of training before any overseas combat assignment."

"What's the paper?" I asked.

The young captain smiled, somewhat mischievously. "I'm not going to tell you. If I did, you probably wouldn't sign it."

I thought for only a few moments with visions of heavily-defended Japanese islands in the Pacific uppermost in my mind. Then I took the paper and, without reading it, signed my name.

My captain friend obviously had a sense of humor. He stood up, shook my hand, and informed me, "Congratulations, Wellborn. You have just volunteered for the American Army Ski Troops."

I was numbed by this announcement. I had just signed a document attesting that I was a qualified skier. That paper had been signed by a boy from the piney woods of East Texas who had rarely in his life seen snow and had never seen a pair of skis. But the die was cast, and that decision materially shaped my entire future. Was that light-hearted captain an angel in disguise? Was this an act of grace? It would seem presumptuous of me to say so.

A few days later I stepped off a train into two feet of snow at Camp Hale, located just outside Leadville, Colorado, right below the Continental Divide. When I was interviewed there for assignment, I could do nothing else but tell them my story. Fortunately for me, the people there also had a sense of humor and perhaps more importantly a feeling of expediency.

I was told, "We have had several other men who have ended up here with your kind of experience. It is easier for us to teach you to ski than to go through the process of assigning you somewhere else."

So, for the first six weeks I was at Camp Hale, I did nothing but take ski lessons. At the end of that time I was assigned to a machine gun platoon in Company B, 86th Mountain Infantry. I was to remain there throughout my stay at Camp Hale. My experience there was not nearly so traumatic as my time at Camp Roberts. Although I was one of the last of my comrades to be promoted to the exalted rank of Private First Class, I managed to complete most of my assignments adequately. In fact, I enjoyed some of the training routine, especially the extensive instruction given to us in mountain climbing. I was not a proficient skier, though I did manage to stand up on the slopes (most of the time).

Our training stay at Camp Hale lasted considerably longer than my captain friend at Camp Roberts had predicted. Finally, in early fall 1944, we were alerted that we were to be sent into combat. In the meantime, however, our military leaders had decided that, before going overseas, the division needed "flatland" training to equip us for whatever terrain we might have to negotiate. Accordingly, we were sent to Camp Swift, just outside Austin, Texas, where we were to remain for about three months.

At Camp Swift I was close to home and actually got to visit my family on some weekend leaves. Still an assistant machine gunner, I applied for Officer Candidate School. Despite my undistinguished record my company commander recommended me. I passed all the tests and interviews, but then another obstacle reared its head. At that time the only officer's school open was for the infantry. My visual defects disqualified me, and I remained an assistant machine gunner, destined to carry part of a gun and a lot of ammunition into combat.

Just three weeks before our division was set for overseas embarkation, I was summoned by my superiors and told that I was to become an army clerk. My one qualification was that I could type. Fortunately, I had found my "niche" in the

military system. I went overseas in December 1944 as part of regimental head-quarters. In the ensuing months my promotions came regularly and quickly. I was for a time the regimental sergeant major of the regiment—the highest noncommissioned rank in the army. My regimental commander asked me to write a history of the regiment in combat. In my research for that assignment I spent much time at the front lines and gained a heightened respect for what ordinary men can do when faced with extraordinary challenges. I was offered a field commission as a second lieutenant and refused, for a variety of reasons.

Although, in this period, my military career was markedly more successful than in its previous stages, it was not all a happy experience—far from it. Virtually all the members of my old machine gun squad in Company B were either killed or wounded. Our division took some 13,000 men overseas and lost almost a third of them as killed or wounded casualties. We were part of the Italian campaign, largely a forgotten war in the chronicles of World War II. It was a bloody and costly effort.

I lost close and cherished friends in that combat. On a particular evening, late in the Italian campaign, I sat with my closest friend in a supposedly "safe" area in north Italy. After weeks on the front line, our regiment had been pulled back for rest. A movie had been arranged for us. No theater was available, so the screen was set up in an open field, and we spectators sat on the ground in front of it. I was sitting beside my friend, a brilliant young man, already a published poet. Before the movie we talked together about our future plans. It looked as if the European war would soon be over. We talked about returning to our families, our girlfriends, and our continued education. We made tentative plans to spend time together after the war when we were both civilians once again. The movie began. It was the biography of the American musical composer George Gershwin, and it was called *Rhapsody in Blue*. Hardly ten minutes after the movie began a single German fighter plane came over. It made just one strafing run, spraying its machine gun bullets, and then was gone. We threw ourselves helplessly on the ground. When the plane was gone, I rose from my prone position, vastly relieved that I was unhurt. I turned to speak to my friend. He did not answer. One bullet, just between the shoulder blades, had ended his earthly existence. My friend was gone.

Not many weeks later the European war was over. My division was shipped back to the States, there to await assignment to the proposed invasion of Japan. Then came the atomic bomb and the end of the war. Along the way I had

accumulated a couple of awards and decorations, largely undeserved from my point of view in comparison to what so many of my comrades had done. But on the army's point system of priority for discharge, those awards counted, and I was soon a civilian.

I arrived home just in time to enroll for the winter academic quarter at Baylor, my last term of study required for my bachelor's degree. At the end of January 1946, I graduated. I applied to Harvard University Law School and was accepted for entrance in fall 1946. Meanwhile, desperate for faculty to meet the needs of a flood of returning veterans to the campus, the chairman of the Baylor Political Science Department hired me to teach courses in American government in the spring term. Thus, I remained at Baylor despite having completed my work there. Was that development an act of grace? Given the events that followed, I am inclined to think so.

Those first months back at Baylor after my military service were not happy or peaceful days for me. I had seen too much human suffering and death. I had lost too many young comrades, their lives and potential suddenly ended. It did not make sense to me. I could find no meaning or purpose in my life. At that time, and for many months afterward, I frequently woke in the night in a cold sweat, having experienced awful nightmares that vividly brought back the traumas of wartime combat. I remembered terrible acts of animalistic depravity, committed mostly by the enemy but sometimes, unfortunately, by my own fellow soldiers. Again and again, I sat in that field in North Italy, watching a movie, when suddenly the world ended for my friend. I had achieved my ambition to be accepted as a student at Harvard, but there was no joy in that knowledge. Somehow it was all ashes in my mouth. In a way that I could not understand, I was dogged with a constant feeling of guilt and failure. I did my job and filled my days with continuous activity of one kind or another, but I was a miserable piece of human flesh.

In my final term of study I was required, like all Baylor undergraduates at that time, to attend regular university chapel services. I went reluctantly and paid little attention to what was happening. I dozed off or read, surreptitiously, the campus newspaper. Then, one morning, my attention was caught when a young man in a basketball jacket was introduced to give his Christian testimony. I was impressed by his honesty and sincerity as he told his simple story of faith. Obviously, he was talking about something that was real and vital to him.

In order to supplement my meager financial allowance under the G. I. Bill, I had tried my hand at freelance writing and had managed to get a couple of inconsequential pieces published. It occurred to me that the young man's testimony might be material for a story. When I inquired about him, I discovered that his name was Jack Robinson and that he was a potential and rising star on the collegiate basketball court. He was studying for the ministry. In addition to his athletic and academic activities, he also was the pastor of a tiny mission church in one of the most economically depressed areas of the city.

I attended several of the services in the little mission and listened to him preach. Eventually, I wrote my article. It was to be submitted to Reader's Digest for possible publication. I felt it necessary before submitting the article to check it out with Jack Robinson. I met him, talked at length with him, and we soon became good friends. That meeting set in motion a chain of events that were life-changing for me.

For many months large groups of Baylor students had been praying for some kind of spiritual awakening on the campus. Now they were planning a week of services aimed not just at the student population but at the city as a whole. They had plans to erect a large tent on a vacant lot near the center of town. The services would be unique in several ways. Instead of bringing in a visiting professional evangelist or a seasoned minister, the preaching was to be done by Baylor students, some of them studying for the ministry, others not. Each young man would preach one night during the week. No collections were to be taken at the services, since all expenses would be raised by contributions prior to the preaching week. Student volunteers would cover the city with publicity promoting what was called a "youth revival."

At the time I first met Jack Robinson, he and his friends were involved in planning for this event. Before I left Baylor for military service, I had been employed as a newscaster on the campus radio station that, at that time, had a statewide hook-up. When I returned to Baylor, I resumed this work. For this reason Jack and others asked me to assist with the publicity planning for the evangelistic campaign. In this way I was drawn into the center of the projected revival. I watched with both bemusement and admiration the dedicated, hard-working efforts of the young men and women. I had no real sympathy for what they were trying to do, but I had to admit they were giving the task everything they had.

The first meeting took place on a Monday night. It was a considerable success. The big tent was crowded with people, both town and gown. At the conclusion of the sermon an invitation was given for Christian commitment, and many individuals responded. After the service was over Jack Robinson and several of his friends asked me to go with them to a late-night prayer meeting.

I went along, more out of curiosity than anything else. The group of ten or fifteen people gathered in a Sunday school classroom in the basement of Seventh and James Baptist Church close to the campus (the church I was later to serve as pastor for ten years). In the semi-darkness of the room, the others knelt to pray. I stayed in my seat, profoundly uncomfortable.

I listened to the others pour out their hearts in earnest prayer. I cannot rationally explain my next actions. Almost unconsciously I found myself out of my chair and on my knees. For the first time in years I tried to pray.

What happened then was something that someone who has never had such an experience would likely not understand. I will put it as simply as I can. There, in that late-night prayer session, I was confronted with the power of the living Christ. The Christ-event, about which I had heard and read, suddenly became a vibrant reality in my own life. The compassionate grace of God reached out and enveloped me. I went to that gathering one kind of person and came out of it changed in basic ways that altered the entire future course of my life. In that experience I was not converted to the Baptist church nor to any particular variety of theology. I did not emerge from that event as a theological fundamentalist, a conservative, or a liberal. I became a "Christ-man."

That confrontation took place fifty-five years ago. Through the troubles, problems, vicissitudes, and occasional successes of my subsequent life, I have never for one moment doubted the reality and life-changing nature of that experience. Whatever I am today, I am because at that moment God in his grace reached down and touched me. On the following Thursday evening I gave my testimony in the revival services. I was soon a member of the preaching team in the citywide and church youth revival services that swept, with tremendous impact upon many lives, across the American South. I had found what I wanted and needed—meaning and purpose in life. My nagging sense of guilt was gone. I had no more nightmares. My future was mapped out for me—not in detail, but in terms of basic commitment.

To return to my metaphor of the courtroom and the witness stand, if the prosecuting attorney asked me, "What is the basis of your Christian faith?" I would be constrained to answer in terms of the narrative I have just unfolded. This is, for me, "the truth, the whole truth, and nothing but the truth."

This is my credo—my personal confession of faith. I do not set it out as a pattern for other men and women. God works with each individual in a personal and unique way. This is my way—my story. In the words of Martin Luther, a great hero of the faith, "Here I stand. I can do no other."